THE COTSWOLD WAY

ARCHAEOLOGICAL WALKING GUIDES

TIM COPELAND

Developed with the Cotswold Way National Trail

The History Press

For Caroline and David

Front cover image: Kimsbury Castle at Painswick Beacon. *Kite Aerial Photographs, courtesy of Hamish Fenton*
Back cover image: Hailes Abbey. *Countryside Agency, Graeme Peacock 02-5764*

First published 2013

The History Press
The Mill, Brimscombe Port
Stroud, Gloucestershire, GL5 2QG
www.thehistorypress.co.uk

© Tim Copeland, 2013

British Library Cataloguing in Publication Data.
A catalogue record for this book is available from the British Library.

ISBN 978 0 7524 6728 3

Typesetting and origination by The History Press
Printed in Great Britain

CONTENTS

THE EXPLORATION OF CAMPS AND EARTHWORKS: SOME SUGGESTIONS TO THE READER IN GENERAL AND TO THE AMATEUR IN ARCHAEOLOGICAL RESEARCH IN PARTICULAR

I want you, my reader, to set out upon this enterprise in a spirit of romance, of reverence for the past, to traverse distances and heights in search of these time-worn relics. But you will have to be prepared to walk and climb, for they were not built in all cases for easy access. I have had to walk for hours over the wind-swept tops of hills, but maybe this will add to the value of the enterprise; climbing to the crest of a hill or tramping over breezy downs on the treacherous surface. Having acquired the desire to take up the quest, we must know *what to look for*. I would advise the would-be antiquarian to get copies of one or two useful books and read up on the subject. You will find plenty of interest and, indeed, amusement of a strenuous kind in tracing ramparts as have become overgrown with trees and almost lost to sight in the undergrowth of ages. You will soon acquire a genius and special capacity for spotting outlines against the sky. It will be seen, therefore, that there is no lack of interest, or even a mild degree of excitement in the pursuit of the knowledge desired. And there should be records taken as far as possible – a drawing or a photograph – as such records will be invaluable to those who only know by the way of book lore. You will have acquired zest – a new enjoyment with a reflection of mild adventure into the great open spaces, away from the beaten track and the dusty highway, and face to face with relics of twenty centuries or more back.

E.J. Barrow, *The Ancient Entrenchments and Camps of Gloucestershire*, 1924.

But Cotswold wall stands up and has strength of its own
Blue against the dawn, Sunset's shield, and Time's wonder and crown.

Ivor Gurney (1890–1937), *Cotswold*

INTRODUCTION

The route of the Cotswold Way Trail was first promulgated some fifty years ago by Gloucestershire-area Ramblers, of which Tony Drake of the Cheltenham area and the late Cyril Trenfield of the South Gloucestershire area were principals. During Footpath Week in May 1970, Gloucestershire County Council launched a Cotswold Way route using existing public rights of way for recreational walking. It was not until May 2007 that the present course of the National Trail was designated, with new rights of way being added to

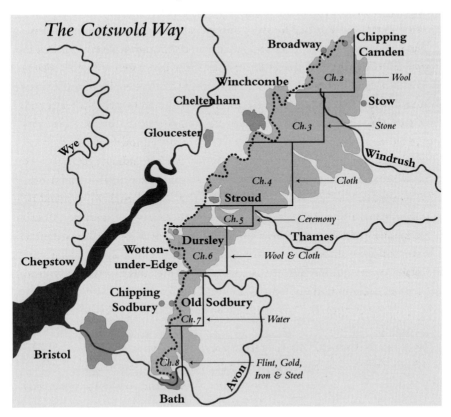

The route of the Cotswold Way and the themes used in the guide.

ensure that the Cotswold Edge could be followed through much of the route. But does this National Trail have an ancient pedigree?

The earliest attempt to see the Cotswold Way as a linear route with an archaeological lineage was in made 1934 when G.B. Grundy, an Oxford Professor of Greek and Roman history with an interest in the landscapes of Gloucestershire, suggested the existence of a prehistoric route following the Cotswold escarpment, which he named the Great Cotswold Ridgeway. His argument was adopted by many historians of the time – primeval forests covered the lowlands and where there was open space, dense mires produced trackless wastes practically un-traversable in wet weather, except for short distances. It was presumed that the higher ground, particularly the ridges, had to be used for long-distance travel, especially as the woodland was thinned out on these crests. Grundy suggested that the origin of the Great Cotswold Ridgeway route was fixed by features such as burial chambers and hill forts which were most concentrated along the ridges, although he gave little thought to the varying dates of these monuments. In 1951 W.F. Grimes proposed a 'Jurassic Way', a corridor along the outcrops of rocks of Jurassic Age of which the Oolitic limestones of the Cotswolds are a part, and along which early movement took place between north-eastern and south-western Britain.

With the intensified application of aerial photography and other archaeological survey techniques since the 1960s, large numbers of prehistoric sites in lowland areas have been discovered, and the concentrations of prehistoric monuments only on the ridges have proved to be largely illusory. It is quite clear that much of the primeval forest had been cleared by the late Bronze Age and, from this period onwards, there were probably local and regional tracks linking these newly emerging communities. Perhaps the situation was very close to what we have today, a multiplicity of upland and lowland local routes, with many intersecting and crossing each other, reflected in footpaths, bridle paths and roads. The routes were composed of swarms of merging, branching, braided, divided, diverging, alternating and re-uniting trackways forming a wide 'webbing', a 'zone of movement', a restless archaeology, which would maintain its general line for centuries. Sections may have been abandoned as the terrain became difficult because of mud, or as a result of the emergence of new centres of importance for trade or power, or for religious reasons, but the general trend remained.

It is likely that the *parts* of the present route of the Cotswold Way National Trail would have had several functions and periods of use depending on their location, and we should not think of it as *all* being used in *all* phases of the past. It was more likely to have been used by 'insiders', those living and working in the locality, rather than 'outsiders' undertaking long journeys along the Cotswold Edge to get elsewhere. It was probably quite a small area that was occupied by the people who used parts of the path *every day*: a Roman villa estate, a medieval civil parish of a small town, village or hamlet, although a Neolithic territory or hill fort hinterland may have been much bigger. People may have used *parts* of the Cotswold route *seasonally* for many reasons: as a Neolithic processional way to the long barrows, a medieval pilgrimage route, a post-medieval packhorse path, a Second World War 'stop-line', observation posts for measuring radiation during the Cold War and, today, a leisure trail. Even if we can't prove archaeological provenance for the whole length of the path, we can acknowledge that in its entirety it traces the 'personality' of past landscapes from pre-history to the present, on both the Cotswolds, the valleys that bite away at them and the lands bordering the Severn. Although it is unlikely that there ever was a Jurassic Way, because of the fundamental influence of the underlying rocks, the Cotswold Way route is certainly a Jurassic way.

Communities in the past are unlikely to have seen or understood places in a vacuum; existing histories, perhaps mythical, defined aspirations and hopes and these were embodied in the landscape and the paths cutting through it. This would be especially so with the views across the landscape from along the Cotswold Edge, enabling people to see the awesome River Severn and the horizon with its iconic shapes of hills, and these factors were probably hugely important in where their monumental structures were placed. People throughout the past, as well as in the present, have revered the view and existing monuments. We know that travellers in the late Iron Age, Roman and medieval periods respected Neolithic long barrows, or the Bronze Age *tumuli*, by not opening or damaging them, and indeed being interred in them as later 'satellite burials'. It wasn't until the Victorian period that, as Dr Garrett commented of Belas Knap in 1919, 'the barrow, after remaining nearly intact through many generations that was continued from era to era, was opened to satisfy the cravings of archaeological curiosity in the years 1863–4'. The continuing significance of the Neolithic long barrow to twenty-first-century visitors is evident at Hetty Pegler's Tump in the number of coins, tea lights and crystals in the cracks between the stones.

The *act* of walking the Cotswold Way is of crucial importance. It is a kind of pursuit, a tracking of a physical trail of someone's path through the past, a following of footsteps. All of this makes the path a place where time 'collapses' and different periods co-exist, flowing at different speeds, enshrining different worlds: the walker 'surfs' time. If a path is made by movement and it measures time with the accumulated footprints of its users, then each walker makes their own Cotswold Way. The path may be public property, but it is also deeply private and forms part of each walker's personal history and archaeology, an elastic string between the recent and distant pasts – we are all 'embedded' in this landscape. This book is really 'Tim Copeland's Cotswold Way', enhanced by the fact that I have lived close to the River Severn and its estuary for a significant portion of my life and walked the hills and sea banks on both sides, always looking at the other. If it is true to say that you can't remember time, only the places in which time occurred, the views from the Cotswold Edge are for me a vast memory bank. I have chosen to 'walk' from Chipping Campden to Bath, not only because it is the direction followed by Anthony Burton's *Cotswold Way: the Official National Trail Guide*, but because I like to see the River Severn opening up. My constant companion was George B. Witts, who published his *Archaeological Handbook of the County of Gloucester* in 1883. There are also accounts of other people's experience, such as the passionate Edward J. Burrow, whose illustrations are used throughout the book, or the tragic Gloucestershire poet Ivor Gurney, quoted on the dedicatory page, as they walked along various lengths of the Cotswold Way route in the past. I hope that their enthusiasm and mine will demonstrate that the path is a part of the vibrant environment into which our ancestors and we are woven. It is being in this shared landscape that is one of the deepest of all historical experiences. Enjoy!

ACKNOWLEDGEMENTS AND SOURCES

Writing this book has been a very different experience from compiling a route guide to the Cotswold Way that shows the itinerary as 'inscribed' on the present landscape. I have attempted to give 'time-depth' to the route and to see how people in the past are 'embedded' in the contemporary landscape: old texts written on the present terrain. Because of the nature of the book, walking alone was not really an option as I needed to know how others reacted to the different type of archaeological sites and monuments, the questions they asked, how effective my explanations were, how *they* became 'embedded' in the land-scape. Caroline Dulake (and Eddie) and David Coles were both essential, but separate, companions. From June 2011 until June 2012 they transported me to different parts of the route and supported me with their own enthusiasm for what they saw. It was interesting to walk the same stretch of the Way at differ-ent times with each and to get often contrasting perspectives on the historic and present landscape. I also enjoyed walking the route at various times with Helen Kealey, Sharon Laycock and Margaret Devers. James Blockley, National Trails Officer for the Cotswold Way, gave much support in the development of the text and in providing illustrations. I am grateful to Ben Roberts, formerly of the British Museum and now of the University of Durham, for access to the Lansdown Gold Disc and for discussions about further directions for research. Richard Savage advised me on the latest position at Crickley Hill. David Wilson kindly allowed me to use material on Wortley Villa before publica-tion and Alan Strickland helped with the post-Second World War monuments. Louise Clough and Lorna Scott of the Bristol and Gloucester Archaeological Society library helped with locating source materials.

SOURCES

There is always a tension between using full academic sources for a walking guide, which might make it unwieldy for the walker to carry, and just suggesting portals through which the user can follow up their own research. It is not an argument that can be decided, as different users will want different things. However, I have decided that just as walkers along the Cotswold Way are adventurous in their walking they will continue to be so in following up the details of individual sites by locating further sources. The quality of information on each site and monument will depend on who excavated it and when, for whom, whether the results were published and, if so, in what detail. Except where specifically stated, the websites of the Transactions of the Bristol and Gloucestershire Archaeological Society and the Annual Journal of the Gloucestershire Society for Industrial Archaeology contain papers on the various sites and monuments. Both have indices and 'find' facilities which could be accessed while walking or afterwards.

The more general English Heritage site www.pastscape.org.uk has been invaluable in the writing of this guide as it summarises previous studies and can be used to identify further references to the monuments. All the dimensions of the sites are taken from this source. The Historic Environment Records are available for enquiries at the Archaeology Services of Gloucestershire and South Gloucestershire, as well as the Heritage Services of the Bath and North Somerset County Councils. The descriptions of the medieval small towns along the route owe a great deal to the research carried out by these bodies as part of the English Heritage funded Historic Towns Surveys of the 1990s.

The website for the Cotswold Way can be accessed at www.nationaltrail. co.uk/cotswold/ where a wide variety of information on other aspects of walking the route can be found. George Witts' *Archaeological Handbook of the County of Gloucester* (1883) can be located at: http://penelope.uchicago.edu/Thayer/E/ Gazetteer/Places/Europe/Great_Britain/England/Gloucestershire/_Texts/ WITGLO★/home.html. Many of the line illustrations are from Burrow, E.J. *The Ancient Entrenchments and Camps of Gloucestershire* (Burrow and Co. Ltd, 1924). The circular walks around Cleeve Hill can be made richer with Garrett, J.H. *From a Cotswold Height: A Description of Country Scenes in Gloucestershire* (J.J. Banks and Son, 1919, reprinted by Sutton Publishing Ltd, 1988). Rawling, Eleanor M., *Ivor Gurney's Gloucestershire: Exploring Poetry and Place* (History Press, 2011) provides deep insights into the music and writings of the ill-starred poet.

This book is not is an architectural guide to the route, so neither the thirty parish churches along the Cotswold Way route (and perhaps sixty within 5 miles either side), nor the country houses along the course, are discussed in any detail.

As up-standing monuments they are a significant part of the landscape and the description of the architectural detail is done superbly well in the *Pevsner* guides to each of the counties through which the way runs. Of course, each structure will have its own guidebook or pamphlet available at the location.

GEOLOGY

The Cotswold Way varies in height along its 164km (102-mile) route, from near Broadway Tower at 312m (1,024ft) to Cleeve Hill, the highest point, at 330m (1,083ft), and 230m (754ft) at Prospect Stile on Lansdown above Bath. These heights produce the stunning views that are the major attraction of walking the Cotswold Way. The rocks that form the Cotswold escarpment are made up of three different geological stages of the Jurassic period and date from 210–140 million years ago. The Lower (earliest) Jurassic resulted in the Lias Group at the base of the series, the clays and silts making up the bulk of the lower slopes. These clays were deposited by wind and wave on the floor of a deep, warm tropical seaway that occasionally shallowed to produce sand banks, lagoons and emergent land influenced by numerous changes in sea level. This formed a complicated variety of rock types seen in the discontinuous layers of limestones and sandstones.

The junction between the lower and middle Jurassic rocks marks a change from the rapidly subsiding Liassic basin into a relatively stable environment. In the middle Jurassic the conditions in which the silts and clays were formed gave way to warm, tropical, shallow seas, much like those around Bermuda today, allowing life to flourish and leaving abundant fossil remains. The rocks that resulted are known geologically as Cotswold Inferior and Great Oolitic Limestones. These Oolitic limestones are made up mostly of ooliths (or ooids), which are sand-sized particles that have concentric rings of calcium carbonate. These rings formed around grains of sand or shell fragments that were rolled around on the shallow sea floor, gathering layer after layer of limestone that shifting tidal currents sculpted into large submarine dunes. Plate tectonics then transported these rocks northward over the past 150–200 million years to their present position. At a later time these rocks were tilted so that a 'regional dip' of the Jurassic strata has formed the wide tablelands of the mid- and northern-Cotswold plateau, which falls gently away south-eastwards with the rivers Evenlode and Windrush etched into it until they meet the plain of Oxford and the Thames.

Weathering and erosion have sculpted the scarp back to its present location over many millions of years through the action of ice sheets. There are spectacular landslips along the Cotswold escarpment caused by slumping and solifluction in the intense freezing and melting cycles ahead of glaciers in the last Ice Age. Often a slab split from the inferior Oolitic limestone outcrop at the top of the escarpment and slid down, coming to rest at various levels. Subsequent weathering and burial by soil creep has made the rounded, low grassy hummocks perhaps a metre or two high and several metres long, but beneath these the limestone slab is hidden.

ARCHAEOLOGY

A major part of the recent weathering and erosion process are those accumulated human footprints embossed on the route of the Cotswold Way making it a 'story line', a biography in rock, and the sites along it are the narratives of past peoples which archaeologists recount through the chronology and the character of places where the events occurred.

The commonly agreed dates used in this guide are

Palaeolithic 500,000 BC–10,000 BC
Mesolithic 10,000 BC–4000 BC
Neolithic 4000 BC–2200 BC
Bronze Age 2200 BC–700 BC
Iron Age 700 BC–AD 43
Roman AD 43–410
Early Medieval 410–1066
Medieval 1066–1540
Post Medieval 1540–1901
Modern 1901–present

All the archaeological sites offer unique traces of the lives of individuals and communities at particular periods in the past, but there are some types that re-occur along the trail, indicating shared needs, beliefs and ambitions.

LONG BARROWS

The term 'barrow', derived from Old English *beorg* or *beorge*, means a mound of earth, and Neolithic long barrows are a haunting feature of the Cotswold Way. Of the 500 examples in England and Wales there are 200 in the Cotswold/ Severn region, of which at least twenty lie along the route of the National Trail or in the parishes alongside it. The 'at least' is because some may have been taken back into the landscape, smoothed by weathering and erosion, robbed of their stone for building or 'ploughed out'. The most recent threat is damage by mountain bikes. The form of structure appears abruptly around 3800 BC and the main concentration of construction is between 3600 BC and 3300 BC. Individual barrows appear to have been utilised at most for a few centuries, but by around 2600 BC few were in use. The Cotswold-Severn tradition of long barrows comprises a stone-built chamber within a rectangular or trapezoidal earthen mound. The siting of these structures is unlikely to have been haphazard, and their locations might have been related to a number of possibilities. They may be on the site of devotion of previous itinerant hunter-gatherers of pre-farming periods, with actual or mythological ancestors remembered through oral histories or genealogies and used to validate an individual group's territory at a time when land was not owned. Many of the Cotswold Edge barrows are visible for long distances and this must have been especially so with the yellow Oolitic limestone showing when newly erected. Some structures may have been sited according to particular landscape features or, more likely, a celestial event such as the mid-summer or mid-winter sunrise or sunset. Each long barrow was laid out in a specific direction: 75 per cent of the Severn-Cotswold tradition is located on a south-west–north-east axis with the only other marked preference being north-south. A simple explanation for this alignment might be to do with protecting ceremonies in the horned courtyard from the prevailing south-west wind which can be vicious on the scarp top.

Some idea of the aspirations of these communities can be gauged by the effort they put in to providing stone palaces for the dead in a timber-based society. Evidence from excavation indicates that stone tools and antler picks were used for quarrying, but there must have been many bio-degradable materials including wooden wedges, levers, rollers, stays, struts, rakes, timber, leather (or wicker) baskets, ropes etc. The excavation of Hazleton North long barrow on the Cotswold plateau suggested that 8,000–14,500 man hours might have been needed to construct it. This could have been in the form of forty people in a single session working more or less continuously for eight hours a day, for between twenty-two and forty-nine days depending on the size of the barrow. An alternative might be that a community of twenty to thirty individuals should be able to raise a team of six able-bodied men for two to three months over five years. Even large capstones of about half a tonne would take only six people to put in position. This indicates that building a long barrow should have been within the capabilities of an extended family group.

The various designs suggest communities demonstrating individuality and autonomy, and not being controlled by an overall authority. Lateral barrows

1 Uley Long Barrow Entrance. *Edward J. Burrow, 'Ancient Entrenchments and Camps of Gloucestershire', 1924, p. 9*

such as Belas Knap have chambers entered from the sides, whereas Hetty Pegler's Tump is a fine example of a terminal barrow with chambers leading off an entrance passage in the heart of the mound. Outside both types of barrow are horned courtyards, which appear to be public spaces with open access and where pits are often found with cattle or pig bones in them. These might be offerings associated with feasting and it is also possible the bones were attached to the stones above or either side of the entry passage, and acted as totems of the group. The walls of the courtyard façade would intensify and heighten the sound, which would contrast with the silence inside. We should not presume that the long barrow entrances were intended only for outsiders looking *in*; they could possibly also have been for the ancestors looking *out*.

In lateral barrows the entrance passage had a small opening that restricted access and required squeezing. But this was not like entering a natural cave system – these places were cleverly designed and built by humans. The overlapping slabs that form the roof were carefully positioned and the large upright stones artistically placed to frame the cells on either side of the entrance passage. Some of the stones have natural hollows and holes,

2 Uley Long Barrow Interior. *Edward J. Burrow, 'Ancient Entrenchments and Camps of Gloucestershire', 1924, p. 9*

perhaps fossilised plant roots made during the rock's formation, and would have been carefully chosen. Jambs in the walls restricted the view into the interior and access to the chambers was physically constrained by stone sills in front of them, demarcating the spaces between entrance passage and the chambers. There is a feeling of passing from one environment into another, perhaps from darkness to light, sound into soundlessness – a metaphor for the journey from life to death. The whole experience was highly claustrophobic and, along with the damp atmosphere and the smell of rotting bodies, must have made for a very frightening and stomach-churning event. Traces of burning within the entrance zone and the chambers indicate the use of torches to give light, and perhaps to hide the smell of the rotting corpses. However, while long barrows are often see as lonely and malevolent places, a visit to Belas Knap in June often sees it covered with golden buttercups, bird's foot trefoil and white campion, making the mound stand out in the landscape.

The chambers themselves have dis-articulated skeletons, demonstrating multiple collective burials, and indicate that the primary purpose of the spaces was to curate human remains. All the evidence suggests that we are dealing with the vaults of family groups and the numbers in the individual tombs are similar to those who were needed to build the long barrows. Often the bones from the same person are scattered in both entrance and chamber zones, suggesting movement within and in the direction of the entrance and subsequently into the outside world. There are usually very few complete skeletons presented, with skulls less common than major limb bones, and this suggests that body parts have been removed either before or after being placed in the barrow. If bones were missing before the skeletons were inserted into the tomb, then there must have been some form of 'skeletonisation'. An explanation for this behaviour might lie in the process of excarnation, where bodies were allowed to rot in the elements either by being raised up on some sort of platform, stored in a box, wrapped in cloth or even sat outside the barrow – there have been so few excavations of archaeological deposits in the areas immediately around the long barrows that there is very little evidence for any of these possible procedures. Corpses may have been inserted into the entrance zones and left to decompose, and moved further into the interior as they became more skeletonised. Whatever the process for removing the flesh was – and it may have varied from community to community or at different periods of time – it is clear that some of the bones were moved around the chambers and then the selective removal of body parts took place and were deposited elsewhere. The culmination of the death – soul loosening – resurrection process might well have happened on special days of the year, possibly connected with the season, celestial events or a 'family' gathering. As yet it is not possible to suggest scientifically through DNA what happened to these bones, especially how far they travelled, though human material has been found on excavated domestic sites. It has been posited that these parts of the ancestors might have been kept in the houses where they had lived – the spirits of the deceased returning to the house of birth or their ancestors and playing a part in the cycle of life.

During the same period, 'causewayed enclosures' appeared in the landscape whose characteristic feature is the presence of frequent breaks or causeways in the boundary ditch. Some of these are entrance gaps, but most are simply narrow blocks, dug as a series of pits rather than a continuous ditch, each perhaps the efforts of a particular family group. Despite this common technique of construction, they were not all built for the same purpose. Some appear to have been defending settlements while others appear to be ceremonial sites, perhaps associated with periodic fairs or gatherings. Certainly one appears at Crickley Hill and a doubtful one close by at Birdlip (or Peak) Camp.

ROUND BARROWS

The word *tumulus* (plural *tumuli*), used on Ordnance Survey maps, is Latin for 'mound' or 'small hill' and usually relates to round barrows. Around 2500 BC individual burials under a round barrow appear in the landscape, the change being an expression of a new belief system with a shift in focus from the community ancestry of the Neolithic to a new social hierarchy, where the lives of individuals were celebrated after death. These forms of burial also suggest that wealth was being accumulated in individual hands rather than in the community and that society was becoming stratified so that a wealthy segment broke surface for the first time.

At their simplest, round barrows are hemispherical mounds of earth and/or stone raised over a burial placed in the middle; these form the majority of those along the Cotswold Way. The sacred area was defined by a circular ditch from which the material for the barrow came. Between them were often stone kerbs to keep the mound material from slipping back. Construction methods range from a single creation process of heaped material to a complex depositional sequence involving alternating layers of stone, soil and turf, with timbers or wattle used to help hold the structure together. The central burial may be placed in a stone chamber or cist, or in a cut grave. Both intact inhumations and cremations placed in vessels can be found and many round barrows attracted 'satellite' burials inserted into the mound at a later date. In some cases these occur hundreds, or even thousands, of years after the original barrow was built and were placed by entirely different cultures.

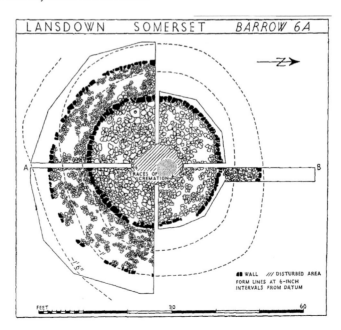

3 Lansdown Round Barrow 6A plan. *Audrey Williams 'Bronze Age Barrows on Charmy Down and Lansdown', Somerset Antiquaries Journal, Vol. 30, 1959, p. 38*

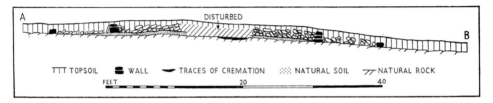

4 Lansdown Round Barrow 6A section. *Audrey Williams 'Bronze Age Barrows on Charmy Down and Lansdown,* Somerset Antiquaries Journal, Vol. 30, 1959, p. 38

Because of the round barrows' unpretentious construction, they are easily ploughed out or form easy targets for stone clearance. Many have been what might today be called 'looted' as it was easy to excavate down through the centre of the structure. E.M. Clifford, concluding her excavation of the Woodchester Ivy Farm Barrow (itself destroyed in 1928 for stone for the Woodchester Estate), comments about the types of barrows in the area discussed by G.F. Payne, writing in 1870. He lists eight round barrows in the Stroud area that he had excavated or whose excavation he researched, including one at Minchinhampton that was dug by the occupier of the land because he dreamed it contained a crock of gold (in fact, he only found that the central portion consisted of fine mould in which there were a few fragments of bronze). Of these eight barrows only one was made of stone, three had fine earth in some quantity in the centre, only one contained a pit below ground level and all had some evidence of burning. For grave goods, flints were found in four barrows, pottery in five, bronze in two and identifiable animals in three. Two had secondary Saxon internments, but there was no evidence of Roman burials. The fine earth may well be the result of processes noted by G. Rolleston in 1876, in his *Notes on Prehistoric Internments of the Cotteswold District,* as 'free access to rain and carbonic acid, to say nothing of rodents and carnivores, and the larvae of insects, all of which animals learn, and act upon the learning, the value of human bone'.

HILL FORTS

Hill forts appear forcibly 'stamped' on the landscape, and even if they have been softened by weathering and their ditches have lost their sharp outline, their banks have collapsed and any vestige of stone or timber work defences has vanished a long time ago, they still dominate the highest and most spectacular hills along the Cotswold Way. It is thought that they first appeared towards the end of the Bronze Age, and proliferated during the early Iron Age. The great majority seem to have been built during the fifth and sixth centuries BC, but most of these were abandoned around 400–350 BC.

On the Cotswold Edge just over half of the sixteen possible hill forts on the route use the escarpment as two sides of a designated area (promontory) and have one circuit of ditch or bank (univallate), while others are contour forts around a high point often having two or more circuits (bi/multivallate). There does not seem to be a relationship between the number of lines of bank and ditches and the area that they enclose, seen for example in the bivallate forts of Cleeve Cloud Camp (1.2ha; 3 acres) and Uley Bury (13ha; 32 acres), compared to the univallate fort at Nottingham Hill which covers 48.5ha (120 acres). Univallate forts are thought to be earlier than the 'developed' multivallated ones, and there may have been three to four hundred years between the time when many of the simple forts were abandoned and that when the survivors became bi/multivallate. It may be that this development marks a major change in Iron Age societies' lifestyles, but what is unclear is the motivation behind such a shift. It could be that one hill fort replaced another through a process of consolidation of communities.

The great diversity of hill fort characteristics suggests that it would be unlikely that along the Cotswold Way there was one moment when all the hill forts were occupied, or that there is only one social explanation adequate for the range of sizes, and therefore the possible population involved. Most recently the idea of the defensive nature of the ramparts, and natural defences, has been dismissed since many univallate forts appear unfinished, do not have any defence in depth and their entrances are simple and overall not suitable for a military role. Even if connected with warfare it is highly unlikely that without a source of water – and most Cotswold Edge hill forts are above the spring line – they could survive a determined siege. The bulk of the evidence suggests

5 Uley Bury Camp. *Edward J. Burrow, 'Ancient Entrenchments and Camps of Gloucestershire', 1924, p. 113*

that hill forts would in many respects have been symbolically defensive rather than practically so, and warfare was primarily about being threatening to your enemies rather than entering into open conflict with them. The effort put into a large fort such as Little Sodbury Camp would have contained messages about the strength and ambitions of the local population and its group pride in digging ramparts. This demonstration of a sense of social unity might have deterred aggression. The presence of a ditch does not necessarily indicate a military role; it might be that a ditch is the result of providing soil for a bank. Many of these enclosures may have had agricultural roles, acting as secure cattle corrals for sheltering and managing livestock, and the smaller ones might have been little more than individual farmsteads. Most of these enclosures could never have contained the numbers of people involved in building and maintaining them and there is abundant evidence from the study of aerial photography for farms and fields on the land below, but unfortunately little work has been done on the relationship between the forts and the Cotswold landscape.

As part of a wider landscape, hill forts might be interpreted as being used for season gatherings, agricultural fair grounds or centres of markets and exchange, where it makes sense to have a consolidated system so that more potential customers could gather at any one time. The idea that some hill forts performed ceremonial functions is not a new one, and at Crickley hill fort the proximity of a long barrow and a Neolithic causewayed camp suggests tradition and the appropriation of ancestral power. There is considerable evidence elsewhere of the existence of shrines and temples within the defences, and the finds of Roman coins in many hill forts suggests a continuity of sacred space before Christianity located its places of worship in the villages below.

THE MEDIEVAL SMALL TOWNS

Historically, the majority of medieval small towns have their origin in the tenth to fourteenth centuries, although Winchcombe already had the administrative organisation in place from its Saxon past. First royal and then secular and ecclesiastical landlords began to promote existing villages to urban status, or to found completely new towns on virgin sites. These developing small towns housed large clusters of the population, and many stood at important road junctions or river crossings, thereby attracting artisans and merchants who found that the towns presented opportunities as a centre of industrial development. One of the main influences in the development of the small towns along the Cotswold Way was the foundation of a market after grant of a royal charter, either to an individual or corporate landowner such as the church – Chipping

Campden around 1180, Broadway 1196, Winchcombe by 1086, Painswick 1253, Dursley 1471/2, and Wotton-under-Edge in 1252, Stroud was only granted market status in 1570–1607. The main motivation was the exploitation of commerce, trade and revenues in the form of markets, taxes and tolls.

The large market area was triangular or square, or formed by widening the main street to allow stalls to be set up along its length. Often specialised buildings such as market houses, lock-ups, market crosses and other structures connected with law and order (such as stocks and/or tumbrils), were constructed for the town's use on market days. Other structures connected to the raw-wool trade are seen in the Woolstaplers' Halls, where Italian merchants were permitted to buy either at the summer fairs or in advance, thereby reserving the clip while still on the sheep's back. The rest of the export trade was regulated by channelling it through the single staple-port of Calais.

In addition to the foundation of a market, many landlords attempted to promote existing villages to borough status. The grant of a borough charter conferred a number of privileges of administrative character, the most important of which was the right to burgage, or freehold tenure for a rent paid to the landlord. This led to the development of specialised town plans, with continuous rows of houses alongside the main roads through the settlement and the 'burgage plot' – long, thin strips of land extending back from the main street which allowed as many burgesses as possible access to the street frontage and gave them the right to put out stalls on market days and to trade, and thus gain income. Each burgage plot had a long and narrow back plot for gardens for food, workshops for small-scale industry and storage. Human and other waste was usually disposed of in pits dug into the garden area. Running behind the burgage plots was a 'back lane', the name still surviving in many small towns in modern streets. The inhabitants of the urban area frequently possessed the means to build more costly and varied houses than were found in the surrounding countryside.

One of the main ways in which landlords flaunted their wealth is seen in the churches. On the northern part of the Cotswold Way, Winchcombe church was being rebuilt in the 1460s, and the main transformation of Chipping Campden probably started around 1450 and continued to the end of the century. Large contributions from rich wool-masters and clothiers like Walter Bradway at Chipping Campden were probably valuable for launching new campaigns of building, reviving existing programmes ailing from lack of money and ensuring continuity of work for several years. Such funding was often paid in instalments, but often the contributions of benefactors are overplayed and money was raised by the collection of gifts in kind from parishioners of every rank, or through wills.

A SCULPTED LANDSCAPE

At the base of the Cotswold escarpment the land has been used for arable agriculture for many thousands of years, and this often produces spectacular patterns in the landscape, particularly the corrugated ridge and furrow and the features known as strip lynchets. The key factor in their creation was the design of the medieval plough, which consisted of a beam supporting a coulter that cut the sod vertically, a share cutting horizontally and a mould board which turned the soil over. The plough team consisted of oxen in pairs (up to eight, at least 12m – 40ft – in length) with the ploughman and a man or boy to encourage the oxen. Clockwise ploughings with the mouldboards of the plough turning the soil towards the centre of the ridge would establish, or increase, the domed section across it and the crest of the plough ridge could stand up to 1m (3ft) high.

In the course of ploughing, small quantities of soil were carried forward by the plough, and when it was lifted and turned at the end of each strip, a small amount of soil was dropped or the ploughman would pause at the end of a furrow and scrape clay from the coulter and mouldboard to speed progress. Eventually, substantial ridges of soil would accumulate in these ways to form long smooth hummocks or headlands. The plough team could be of considerable length, and problems could develop in getting the plough to the end of the strip without trampling the crop in the adjacent furlong. The solution was to turn the team at the end of the strip well before the headland was reached, before turning back down it. This turn to the left, while still pulling the plough, is represented in the reverse 'S' shape of a typical ridge. Often over a long period it can turn into a 'C' configuration. The most common explanation of ridge and furrow is that it facilitates good drainage as slopes of more than five degrees tend to have ridge and furrow at right angles to the contours which empty into streams and rivers. During the nineteenth century, a mechanised form of ploughing involved hauling a plough between steam engines, though the ridges were quite narrow and completely straight and did not have the reverse 'S' shape associated with medieval ploughing with oxen.

Strip lynchets, features with long parallel terraces usually running along the contours in stepped flights with ramps for access, are commonly seen on steep hillsides along the Cotswold Way, especially above Wotton-under-Edge and along the escarpment to the south, most spectacularly at Hinton Camp (centred on ST 741 764) and Cold Ashton (ST 744 721). Several explanations have been put forward for their date and purpose: they have been attributed to the middle Iron Age because of their proximity to hill forts and Roman and medieval vineyards have been popular conjecture, especially as the lynchets

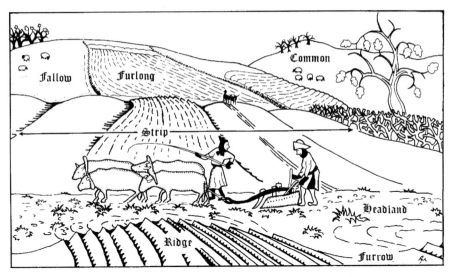

6 The medieval countryside. *After Richard Muir 'Shell Guide to Reading the Landscape', 1981, p. 99*

face south or south-east in the direction of the sun's course. The most logical explanation is that strip lynchets are fossilised field systems of medieval date and are an extension of the normal open fields onto steep ground. They are a combination of repeated episodes of ploughing of a smooth slope in a consistent direction, cutting steps into the hillside. The arduous efforts to form plough terraces would not have been countenanced by communities which enjoyed adequate resources, so strip lynchets are associated with over-population and land hunger when suitable low-lying ground was in short supply or non-existent.

In some places, such as above Stancombe House and extensively on West Littleton Downs at the southern end of the route, 'Celtic fields' are to be seen (although with more clarity from an aircraft than from the ground). These are small square or rectangular fields usually bounded by lynchets, originating in the Bronze Age, but widespread in Romano-British times throughout the British Isles.

Woodland

Just as soils were the major factor in the development of wool production on the plateau, they also play a determining role in the landscape on the scarp slopes and in the valley below. Examining the Ordnance Survey maps along the route of the Cotswold Way, it is obvious that there are significant areas of woodland cascading from the commons above. These are the remains of much more extensive woods which have been eaten into for agricultural land since the Middle Ages. The steepness of the escarpment has ensured their survival, as the Jurassic limestones are too steep, and the soils they produce too poor, to be worth the considerable effort of using strip lynchets. On the stretch of the Cotswold Way between Great Witcombe Roman Villa and Painswick Beacon are Rough Park Wood, Pope's Wood and Kite's Wood, all part of the Cotswold Commons & Beechwoods National Nature Reserve. The incised valleys behind Wotton-under-Edge, Alderley and Hawkesbury also have similar curtains of woodland.

The escarpment woodlands are made up of closely planted beech trees that, on maturity, produce straight boles with an understorey of yew, holly and box; they have now generally developed a high-forest structure. Each of these species is slow growing and indicates that the beechwoods are undoubtedly of natural origin. However, the woodlands have a long history of management for timber, largely through coppicing, a traditional method of woodland management which takes advantage of the fact that many trees make new growth from the stump or roots if cut down, producing branches which were used for everyday life, farmyard implements, fences and utensils, with the under wood being used for domestic fires. Some presently mature beech trees were the shoots last coppiced before the First World War. Between the trees, straight wood banks can be seen, which indicate ownership in the medieval period. Close to Bath, ash becomes the dominant tree on the steep slopes. Single trees in field hedges were probably planted in the nineteenth century.

THE SECTIONS OF THE WALK

SECTION 1

WOOL
CHIPPING CAMPDEN TO WINCHCOMBE

The Cotswold Way travels through every aspect of the wool trade, from the raising of sheep to the manufacture of woollen cloth. Areas underlain by the Oolitic limestone forming the Cotswold plateau were ideal for sheep and had extensive tracts of open grazing – downs, sheep walks and heaths. Large flocks could be grazed here by day and folded by night on the open fields, thus ensuring a continuous flow of nutrients that kept these thin, easily leached soils in heart. Finds from prehistoric sites and Roman villas and towns indicate that sheep and wool have been an important part of the Cotswold economy for a very long time. At Chedworth Roman villa, in the 'Seasons' mosaic, winter is dressed in a *Birrus Britannicus* (British cloak), a hooded cloak made of wool; the Diocletian Price Edict (AD 301), which set the maximum prices for goods throughout the Empire, not only levied a huge tax on it but also set the price at 6000 denarii, the equivalent of buying 660lbs (300kg) of pork or 110gals (500l) of wine. One of the main English exports up to the fourteenth century was raw wool, which was shipped to the continent where it was made into finished cloth to be sold back to England. Michael Drayton, writing at the end

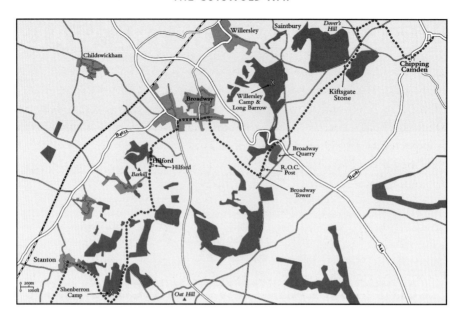

Wool: Chipping Campden to Stanway.

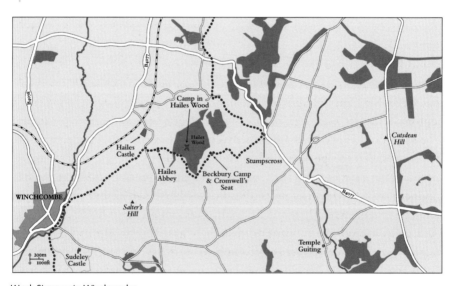

Wool: Stanway to Winchcombe.

of the sixteenth century, suggests that Cotswold wool was very fine: 'it comes near that from Spain for from it a thread might be drawn as fine as silk'. The Abbot of Gloucester was shearing 10,000 sheep, and it was probably to store wool-clip as well as corn that, around 1300, he built the great barn still standing at Frocester. Another splendid barn was erected in Stanway by the Abbot of Tewkesbury. John de Gamages, Abbot of Gloucester 1284–1306, increased the abbey flock to 10,000 sheep, producing 46 sacks of wool for market in one year. In the last decades of the thirteenth century the Bishop of Worcester enlarged his flock at Bishop's Cleeve from 700 to 1,000 and at Blockley from 800 to 1,312. In the early fourteenth century Pegolotti, a Florentine, drew up a list of the annual yields of wool from English and Scottish religious houses, of which there were 202. Winchcombe Abbey was one of only twelve that could be expected to provide forty or more sacks of wool each year, implying that the abbey owned around 8,000 sheep and gained an income of about £350 per annum from the trade.

CHIPPING CAMPDEN (CENTRED ON SP 151 392)

There is no evidence of either prehistoric or Roman settlement close to the town, and Chipping Campden is first recorded in a charter of around 1005. It is likely that the name means 'valley with enclosures', from *campa* and *denu*, and the prefix 'Chipping' is derived from *ceping*, meaning market or marketplace. The earliest settlement is thought to have stood in the area of the church and site of the seventeenth-century manor house, as it is highly likely that Hugh de Gondeville, the lord of the manor in the late twelfth century, would have founded the borough close to the seat of his power. Although the exact location of the medieval manor house is unknown, it is possible that when Sir Baptist Hicks built Campden House in the early seventeenth century, he reused the site of the medieval manor and, though providing a level of continuity of status, destroyed any remains of earlier structures. It was from this village that the borough was laid out with just a main street, the High Street, which had well defined burgage plots on either side providing income in the form of rents. On the north-west side of the High Street the plan was particularly regular, the burgage plots extending back as far as Back Ends and almost certainly a medieval back lane; on the south-east the plots stretched back to the River Cam. Tolls from the weekly market and annual fair held in the wide, central part of the High Street would also have been advantageous to the manor. (See plate 1.)

Chipping Campden has many of the characteristics of the wool towns across the Cotswold plateau, establishing itself as a major commercial centre for the purchase of wool from the Midlands and Welsh Marches as well as from the surrounding area. It was not a centre for the processing of wool, but concerned itself only with its distribution, and the Woolstapler's Hall, now a private home, is thought to have been built during the early fourteenth century as a meeting place for wool merchants and their principals, or their principals' agents. Infilling of the High Street is likely to have begun in or before the fourteenth century, but the present Market Hall was built by Sir Baptist Hicks in the early seventeenth century, and it is not known whether an earlier market hall existed on the site or elsewhere. By the second half of the fifteenth century, the town's fortunes were at their peak: this is reflected in the parish church, which was originally dedicated to Our Lady, or the Blessed Virgin Mary, and received its present dedication to St James at the time of the Reformation. Although evidence survives for its Norman origins and thirteenth- and fourteenth-century additions, it was during the fifteenth century that the church was extensively rebuilt and extended, with the tower being constructed and the nave added into the existing church.

By 1601 Chipping Campden was no more than a local market centre serving the surrounding area of farms and estates, and cotton and silk began to take the place of wool in men's clothing. A silk mill opened in Sheep Street *c.*1790 and employed a number of women until it closed in 1842. A flax mill also operated in the town until 1838, which employed over forty hands, but its location is unknown. With the increasing use of the railways to transport goods, costs increased and caused the decline of the town's industries. The import of Indian and French silk killed the local industry, and the agricultural slump of the later nineteenth century was the final blow. Chipping Campden's population dropped by a quarter in the last half of the nineteenth century and many houses and cottages were left to fall into ruin.

While Gravel House at its northern end is probably of the fourteenth century, the High Street as it exists today is lined with buildings which date mainly from the seventeenth and eighteenth centuries and indicates periods of rebuilding, re-fronting and infilling of the original tenement plots, although it was not until the nineteenth century that the street frontages came to be built up along their entire lengths. The stone-lipped pit opposite the almshouses was designed for washing carts and soaking their wheels and was intended to replace a pond that stood at the bottom of Church Street.

KIFTSGATE STONE (SP 135 389)

The Kiftsgate Stone stands on the edge of a wood by the side of the road and is 1m (3.2ft) high, 0.7m (2ft) wide and 0.2m (1ft) thick, of unimpressive appearance. The perforation is probably modern, suggesting use as a gatepost, although its present visible length makes it rather short for that purpose. 'Kifts' is thought to derive from Old English '*cyft*', meaning a 'meeting or conference'; hence Kiftsgate would mean 'gate or gap where meetings are held', and it was presumably here that the 'hundred' of Kiftsgate met. The stone was a centre for local and national announcements, including proclamations of the crowning of kings up to William IV.

WILLERSEY CAMP (SP 118 383) AND LONG BARROW (SP 182 328)

While these sites might be tempting to visit, the escarpment here has been much disturbed by quarrying, slumping and the construction of the golf course, which has led to considerable damage. While the Iron Age builders of the hill fort had respected the Neolithic long barrow, in 1884 Witts partially excavated it 'with praiseworthy zeal … with a band of willing workers' on the day previous to a visit by the Bristol and Gloucester Archaeological Society. Some drystone walling was revealed on the north and south sides, and at the east end were large stones and remains of chambers probably displaced by earlier excavators. 'A hearty thanks' was given to the landowner and excavators by the company present!

7 Willersey Camp. *Edward J. Burrow, 'Ancient Entrenchments and Camps of Gloucestershire', 1924, p. 114*

THE VIEW FROM BROADWAY TOWER (SP 114 361)

Broadway Tower itself was built in 1794 by James Wyatt for Lady Coventry, who wondered if a beacon on the hill could be seen from her house in Worcestershire – approximately 35km (22 miles) away. She sponsored the construction of the folly to find out and the exercise was a success, as the inter-visibility was confirmed.

This high point also gives a 360-degree view of the sky over the Midland Plain, the River Severn and the Cotswold plateau, and proved useful in organising the air defences of the South Midlands. In the fenced compound just before you arrive at the tower are two consecutive structures (SP 114 363) used in the network of observation stations post-1945. Experience during

8 Broadway Tower, built in 1794 by James Wyatt for Lady Coventry, who wondered if a beacon on this hill could be seen from her house in Worcester — approximately 35km (22 miles) away. She sponsored the construction of the folly to find out. *Author's collection*

the Second World War suggested that there would be a need for increased protection from enemy aircraft if the United Kingdom was ever faced with war again. Many sites in the defensive system used Orlit 'A' structures manned by the Royal Observer Corps. These provided accommodation in pre-cast concrete panelled structures known as 'Orlit' posts, after the manufacturers Messrs Orlit Limited of Scotland. This particular example was opened in 1950 and contained an observation area with a plotting table and removable roof, as well as a shelter and stores. It retains its original wooden door and wooden instrument mounting and all the GPO wiring is still in place, including a large, circular metal junction box with a large number of terminals.

A second, underground, Royal Observer Corps post was opened in June 1960 and built as part of an extensive network designed to confirm and report enemy aircraft and nuclear attacks on the United Kingdom. It was constructed using a nationally agreed design. A hole approximately 2.7m (9ft) deep was excavated and a structure cast using reinforced concrete. The floor was *c.*30cm (12in) deep and walls approximately 18cm (7in) broad with a roof about 20cm (8in) thick. The whole structure was then sealed with bitumen for waterproofing purposes. An access shaft, doubling as an air shaft, can be seen protruding above ground, and at the opposite end of the structure a further air shaft was created. Two metal pipes, one 13cm (5in) in diameter and the other 2.5cm (1in) in diameter, protrude from the roof, to be used with operational instruments. Above ground, the air vents were covered by downward-sloping louvres, with sliding metal shutters below ground to control air flow in case of contamination by radioactive fallout. There was also a toilet/store. The post was closed in September 1991 after the fall of the Communist Bloc, but is open for visitors at times specified in the Tower. You will meet another example of a nuclear observation post at Horton (ST 766 838), also using the Cotswold ridge for all round visibility. (See plate 2.)

The underlying rocks of the Great Midland Plain in front of you are the flat Triassic sediments laid down in desert conditions some 250 million years ago. You will also see some hills that will accompany you for much of the route

9. Orlit 'A' Royal Observation Corps Post. Experience during the Second World War suggested that there would be a need for increased protection from enemy aircraft if the UK ever faced war again. Many of these sites received pre-cast concrete-panelled structures known as 'Orlit' posts, after the manufacturers of the structures Messrs Orlit Ltd of Scotland. It was opened in the 1950s. *Author's collection*

and become orientation markers. To the left is the whale-backed, hill-forted Bredon Hill, an outlier of the Cotswolds Oolite, dominating the landscape. It was detached from the main escarpment by diverging ice masses coming down from Wales and Lincolnshire. Behind Bredon are the Malvern Hills, the stubborn, hard stubs forming a serrated crocodile lurking over the middle Severn Valley. They are composed of some of the oldest rocks in the British Isles heaved violently up from the depths of the earth's crust. They were crystallised and made hard between 580 and 600 million years ago; previously, *c.*1000 million years ago, they were probably ancient shales and sandstones laid down as sediments. Further to the south-west on a clear day can be seen the sentinel of May Hill with its crowning clump of trees, which will be the landmark that you will see along at least 75 per cent of the route.

Walking down to Broadway you will cross most of the geological sequence. The first part of the scarp is formed by the permeable Inferior Oolite, with the evidence of slumping obvious until the spring line, marked by rushes, indicates the junction with the impermeable clays and silts. Then underlying Liassic rocks produce the much richer soils which have been used for arable agriculture for many thousands of years, here in the form of the ridge and furrow running against the grain of the Cotswold escarpment to drain the fields made damp by the seeping of water from the spring line.

BROADWAY (CENTRED ON SP 100 378)

Broadway lies on sloping land below the Cotswold Edge. The early town would have been fed by streams originating from springs on the scarp slope. There is little evidence for pre-medieval settlement under the modern town, although excavations in the 1940s to the west revealed indications of prehistoric and Roman occupation, and other sites have been identified to the north through aerial photography. The eleventh century (and possibly earlier) focus was probably around St Eadburga's church, 1km (0.6 miles) south of the urban area, and the migration of the settlement to the medieval and present location was probably governed by a major saltway from Evesham to Chipping Norton over the Cotswold scarp and then on towards the south-east, explaining the Anglo-Saxon form of the place name as *Bradanwege*, meaning 'the broad road'.

Broadway has been identified as a medieval new town created by the Abbey of Pershore either in the late twelfth century or mid-thirteenth century, and the medieval street system is still the basis of the modern pattern, as no new streets have been added. Tenement plots have been identified north and south of the marketplace and west of Leamington Road, their limits being deduced by the presence of a Back Lane adjacent to the Tourist Information Offices to the north and the surviving ridge and furrow, which suggests agricultural land. It is probable that these components form the original extent of the planned medieval borough.

The weekly market was first recorded in 1196, and the marketplace is identified as the triangular area at the west end of the High Street (The Green) and the wide High Street as far east as Leamington Road. There are two surviving medieval buildings close to The Green, the Abbot's Grange and the Broadway Hotel, both with timber-framed elements dating to the fourteenth century. At the Grange, documentary records show that as well as the fourteenth-century hall, oratory and chamber that survive as standing buildings, there was a kitchen, gatehouse, stables and bakehouse. There are a handful of other medieval buildings on the High Street, or fragments of such, notably the early fourteenth-century Prior's Manse. (See plate 3.)

The settlement seems to have lost much of its urban status in the sixteenth century. However the sheer extent of the surviving seventeenth-century houses, with new houses built east of the medieval core, suggests that it was relatively prosperous in the seventeenth and eighteenth centuries. The present church was built as a 'chapel of ease' in 1608 and rebuilt as the church of St Michael and All Angels in 1839, although the medieval parish church 1km (0.6 mile) south of the settlement continued in use. Stone seems to have replaced timber-framing as the common building material early in the seventeenth century, if not a little beforehand. The abandonment of the timber-framed technique in construction might be due to changes in taste, increases in the relative cost of timber construction or decreases in the relative cost of stone construction, allied with cheaper stone from the quarries. The turnpike roads were constructed in the early seventeenth century and the coaching trade became important in Broadway, with a number of large inns occupying the High Street. The economy of the then village was based on agriculture, with a minor element of glove-making in the nineteenth century.

Only a few of the seventeenth-century buildings aspire to high status, notably the Lygon Arms, which was built as a large private house but later became an inn. There are a few grander eighteenth-century houses, distinct in their size and their classical style from the slightly older houses. The general pattern along the main street suggests a very gradual decline that, judging from the comparative lack of early and mid-nineteenth-century houses, continued until the latter part of the nineteenth century. The Cotswold vernacular style prevailed throughout much of the eighteenth century and was effectively revived in the latter part of the nineteenth, creating the harmonised appearance much valued by tourists in the present.

BURHILL FORT (SP 084 362)

This early to middle Iron Age enclosure was only discovered in 1960 by L.V. Grinsell, an amateur archaeologist for most of his career, who introduced the tradition of active fieldwork to archaeology when most professionals were concerned only with excavation. It is his work on round and long barrows that forms the basis of their study along the Cotswold Way. The enclosure, which can be reached by a footpath from the main route, is sited on a spur which is cut off from the main escarpment by a single rampart. The hill fort is not in a good defensive position, as the hilltop rises slightly above the fort, meaning that the interior would have been overlooked. The rampart on the north-east side has been partially destroyed by ploughing and extends for only 125m (410ft), less than halfway across. The surviving bank is 7.6m (25ft) wide and up to 2.5m (8ft) high and a possible ditch has been detected, which is 9m (30ft) wide and 0.9m (3ft) deep. The natural scarp appears to form the other two sides of the 5ha (12 acres) enclosed, although a bank on the south-western side running along the top of the spur for 25m (82ft) might be part of the rampart; it is, however, more likely to be a medieval or post-medieval pillow mound for the breeding of rabbits. A scatter of flints indicates a previous use of the spur, and early Iron Age pottery has also been found, as well as a prehistoric saddle quern for grinding corn.

SHENBERROW CAMP (SP 080 334)

The bivallate hill fort on Shenberrow Hill is typical of the small early Iron Age settlements of the Cotswold escarpment in that it was probably inhabited by a small community, perhaps several families. It covers an area of 1ha (2.5 acres) on a sloping spur, with the inner defences consisting of a rampart 9m (30ft) wide and 1.5m (5ft) high and a ditch 8m (25ft) wide and 0.9m (4ft) deep, both features terminating at the scarp edge to the north and south. A bank 6m (20ft) wide and 1m (3ft) high, set parallel with the scarp edge, links the rampart ends, but seems not to have a ditch. Excavations in 1935 (but not published until 1961) showed the inner rampart on the south to have a drystone revetment on its inner face, and a cutting across the scarp-edge bank revealed a core of loose stones. The entrance was through a gap in the rampart at the south. The outer defences are intact on the north side, where the rampart is 8m (25ft) wide and 0.6m (2ft) high, with a ditch 8m (25) ft wide and 1m (3ft) deep. Elsewhere the rampart has been levelled and the ditch can only be seen from the air as a crop mark. In the north corner of the interior of the fort is an undated enclosure 18m (60ft) by 15.2m (50ft), bounded by a narrow bank. Excavations recovered early Iron Age pottery from a probable hut site in the south-west angle of the rampart, together with fragments of iron, a bronze brooch and parts of a rotary quern. Some Roman pottery indicated sporadic occupation of the site no later than the second century AD.

10 Shenberrow Camp. *Edward J. Burrow, 'Ancient Entrenchments and Camps of Gloucestershire', 1924, p. 106*

STANWAY HOUSE, GATEHOUSE, TITHE BARN AND CHURCH (CENTRED ON SP 061 325)

The grouping of manor house, gatehouse, tithe barn and Norman church is a rare survival from the medieval period. Formally owned by the Abbot of Tewkesbury, the manor came into the hands of the Tracy family after the dissolution of the smaller monasteries in 1533.

The landscaped park at Stanway House is one of the few country houses below this section of the Cotswold Way. It was originally a medieval deer park, developed in 1683 but designed as a formal landscape and laid out sometime between 1783 and 1817 by Henrietta Tracy-Keck. Extending mainly to the east, north and north-west of the house, there is principally open parkland with some areas now returned to agriculture, with scattered trees, geometrically arranged clumps and small areas of woodland. The earliest view, published in 1712, shows a walled geometrical garden, walled kitchen gardens, plantations and possibly orchards. A formal garden with a topiary was created to the east of the house in the mid-twentieth century. The present formal gardens were laid out c.1955 by Lady Violet Benson.

11 Stanway House. *Countryside Agency: Jo Ward*

Tithe Barn

The fine tithe barn at Stanway, dating from the fourteenth century or earlier, was built for the Abbot of Tewkesbury and has been converted for use as a village hall.

12 Stanway Tithe Barn. *Countryside Agency: Jo Ward*

St Peter's Church

Although there was a church at Stanway in 1086 it was rebuilt in the twelfth century, and much of the masonry of the nave and chancel is of that date. The tower was added, and a low arch cut in the west wall, in the thirteenth century. The upper part of the tower was rebuilt in the fifteenth century, giving it three stages with gargoyles at the corners, battlements and pinnacles. Some rebuilding took place in the late eighteenth century, when the chancel was altered and probably the east window was replaced. The church underwent considerable rebuilding in 1896, when much of the twelfth- and thirteenth-century masonry was apparently removed.

Gateway

This very attractive gateway is unusually positioned at right angles to the house, presumably because the church was in the way in front of the house. The lodges, either side of the gateway, have narrow bay windows and the whole is topped by shaped gables crowned with scallop shells from the Tracy coat of arms. The archway has fluted columns either side.

Stanway War Memorial

The striking bronze of St George and the Dragon is situated at the south side of the village, at the junction of the B4077 road. It is by Alexander Fisher. The stone column and plinth is by Sir Philip Stott and the inscription was carved by Eric Gill.

STUMPS CROSS (SP 075 303)

This is perhaps a pilgrim's cross on the route between Chipping Campden and Hailes Abbey. It is a rough stone block around 0.6m (2ft) square, from the centre of which protrudes a short stone stump. Pilgrim crosses came about in response to the biblical quotation:

This is what the Lord says: 'Stand at the crossroads and look; ask for the ancient paths, ask where the good way is and walk in it, and you will find rest for your souls.'

Jer. 6:16

13 Beckbury Camp. *Edward J. Burrow, 'Ancient Entrenchments and Camps of Gloucestershire', 1924, p. 52*

BECKBURY CAMP (SP 064 299)

The unexcavated univallate promontory hill fort of Beckbury Camp encloses 2.2ha (5.5 acres) and is sub-rectangular in shape, with rounded corners orientated north–south. The north and west sides of the camp are defined by the steep slope of the escarpment. On the south and the east the bank is about 8m (25ft) wide and rises 1.5m (5ft) above the interior. The bank on the eastern side has been damaged by animals repeatedly passing through a later break in it. The entrance was probably in the south-west, where there is a 14m (45ft) gap between the end of the bank and the edge of the escarpment, although there is a better position on the north-west where there is a hollow way that leads downslope to a number of springs. Many Roman coins of Aurelius (AD 161–180) and Severus (AD 93–211), some flint arrowheads and middle Iron Age pottery have been found here. Drystone revetting is visible in the outer face of the rampart and fire-reddened stones are visible in the outer face of the bank. Evidence of a filled outer ditch is exposed where the ground falls steeply away; the line of the ditch remains visible in the natural rock and continues about 6m (20ft) down the escarpment.

CROMWELL'S SEAT (SP 063 000)

According to local tradition, this is the point from which Thomas Cromwell watched the destruction of Hailes Abbey in 1539. Although there is a record of Cromwell visiting Hailes before the Dissolution, the stone monument is

14 Cromwell's Seat. *Author's collection*

of Classical, rather than Gothic, design. Its domed niche probably containing a statue and the structure is not earlier than the mid-seventeenth century. It may have been put up by the Tracy family of Stanway to mark the limits of their estate or the boundary between Hailes and Stanway parishes.

CAMP IN HAILES WOOD (SP 056 301)

This feature in Hailes Wood is marked on the Ordnance Survey map as an 'earthwork' and has often been interpreted as a small Iron Age settlement 0.8ha (2 acres) in area. While it is in a good position for defence, being on a spur of the Cotswold escarpment the ridges and hollows are more likely to be geological features accentuated by wear on the footpaths through the wood. It has been suggested that the earlier features were adapted and refortified between 1138 and 1150 with work on Hailes Castle, but there is no evidence for this.

HAILES CASTLE (SP 051 301)

The documentary evidence for the castle built at Hailes, around AD 1139–48 is insufficient to establish its exact site, but it probably lay close to the existing twelfth-century church and was destroyed when the abbey was founded in 1246. The moated site can still be traced at a distance of 137m (150yds) due east of the church, and a road, often mistaken for a ditch, can be traced leading across Hailes Field from the direction of the Monk's Pool and the Saltway, to the castle entrance. The moat has now been completely filled in.

HAILES ABBEY (SP 050 299)

The Cistercian abbey of Hailes was founded in 1245 by Richard, Earl of Cornwall, in thanksgiving for his deliverance from a shipwreck. The land was given to him by his brother Henry II. Its site was ideal for a monastery, with the presence of springs, a supply of water and flat land on which to build the church, living quarters and buildings to provide various agricultural activities. More than anything else, it was secluded, being screened by an intervening hill from Winchcombe Abbey, and fitted the Cistercian Statues of Order that it should be 'far from the concourse of men'. The site was sheltered by the wooded slopes of the Cotswold escarpment opening out onto the Vale of Evesham and the Severn Valley, making access to the Forest of Dean possible; indeed, in 1246

King Henry II gave forty oaks from the Forest. There was fertile soil around it suitable for arable farming and orchards, and the Cotswold uplands were ideal for sheep. The springs above the site were used for pure drinking water, and the stream led into the fish ponds and then fed the stone drain which runs beneath the abbey, under buildings through stone-lined conduits and eventually was used in the reredorter to carry off human waste from the site.

The anonymous monastic chronicler of Hailes tells of the monks arriving in June 1246 from their Mother Abbey at Beaulieu and setting 'up their tents at Hailes Mill, each and everyone seeing the roughness of the terrain said "How awful is this place" wondering how from such unpromising beginnings might grow a noble monastery'. By 1251 he was able to say that 'a fine church, adequate dormitory, a dignified frater and a large spacious cloister walk with adjoin buildings' had been erected for dedication.

The abbey was built by 1277, using stone from quarries under the escarpment. The ruined remains are divided between its inner precinct and outer court, which are separated by a boundary that has not survived later landscaping. The inner precinct contains the claustral buildings, of which the walls of the cloister survive mostly at foundation level, although at the south end of the west range three bays survive to full height. To ensure that the cloister received as much sunlight as possible, the abbey church was to the north. Most prominent today is the elaborate ambulatory, with five radiating chapels built in 1270 to accommodate pilgrims who came to see the 'the Holy Blood of Hailes' – allegedly a phial of Christ's own blood brought to Hailes by the Earl of Edmund (d. 1300). A sixteenth-century monk of Hailes described how a shrine was made – 'a noble and rich of gold and silver and precious stones'. (See plate 4.)

A geophysical survey undertaken in 1978 also revealed the infirmary and another building beyond the east range, both of which lay under the spoil from nineteenth- and twentieth-century excavations. The monks' frater has been excavated and consolidated. Drainage operations north of the transept confirmed that a cemetery was in the area. The outer court contains the site of a gatehouse chapel, believed to be in the vicinity of the parish church.

The Cistercians never ate fresh meat in the early Middle Ages, but fish was important as a source of protein, and four fishponds were dug. The sites of two mills and earthworks representing internal boundaries and water management features are visible from the ground and on aerial photographs. Of the ponds, three survive unaltered, while the fourth was landscaped in the seventeenth century and the mills survive as earthwork platforms. On the west side of the monument, in the grounds of Hailes House, is a barn thought to be contemporary with the abbey. A further abbey barn has been revealed by aerial photographs to the north of the parish church. The abbey was dissolved in

1539 and the splendid buildings looted and largely destroyed except for parts of the cloister, which were retained as a dwelling. Later, the buildings were sold to a dealer in monastic properties, soon after which the church was demolished. In the seventeenth century, much of the west range and the abbot's lodging became the home of the Tracy family, until 1729 when the buildings were converted into two farms.

Chaucer, in the Pardoner's Tale of *The Canterbury Tales*, writes: 'By Goddes precious herte' and 'By his nayles, And By the blood of Crist that is in Hayles.' A pilgrim's badge of copper alloy with three figures, the central one tied to a tree and flanked by two archers, was found close to the abbey alongside the Saltway, a track which continues on to Cirencester and then to the River Thames. A similar badge, probably of St Edmund of Bury – also a site of pilgrimage – has been found near the site of the Tabard Inn in London, made famous by Chaucer's *The Canterbury Tales*. Since the hostelry was a traditional meeting point for pilgrims of various origins, bound for numerous destinations, it may be that the owner had come a long way to Hailes. The pilgrim route to Hailes Abbey from Winchcombe (which had no precious relics to attract pilgrimage) is probably that followed by the present Puck Pit Lane.

The parish church at Hailes never grew to a great size as it was overshadowed by Hailes Abbey. The village, recorded in Domesday Book of 1086, was already a century old when the monks arrived and was probably moved to the nearby settlement of Didbrook, where a new church was built for the villagers. However, the church was equipped with a fine set of wall paintings before 1300: wall paintings of the chancel repeat the heraldry of the Abbey including the eagle of its founder Richard, King of the Romans, and castles for Eleanor of Castile, queen of Richard's nephew, Edward I. On the south wall of the nave a wall painting was discovered which shows a huntsman coursing three greyhounds after a hare. The interior has not changed much since the seventeenth century.

WINCHCOMBE (CENTRED ON SP 021 284)

There is little evidence for prehistoric settlement in Winchcombe, although there is an increasing occurrence of Roman finds indicating a significant occupation, possibly a small town. It was during the period from *c.*600 until the Norman Conquest that Winchcombe reached the peak of its importance, as it lay at the centre of a well-defined political and administrative region of Mercia and at a reasonable distance from Tamworth, which was the Mercian 'capital', as well as being accessible to other seats of Mercian power. As the threat of

Danish incursions increased in the later ninth century, King Alfred and his successors constructed a series of *burhs*, fortified settlements, throughout the territories of the West Saxons, and it is likely that Winchcombe's significance at this time led to it being included among these strongholds.

The Anglo-Saxon defences of Winchcombe are thought to have been laid out in the ninth century and to have principally made use of natural features, along with some deliberate construction work. The only visible portion of the circuit follows the southern side of Back Lane, where archaeological excavation demonstrated a 'V'-sectioned ditch with an accompanying bank, possibly laid out on an area stripped of turf. In other *burhs*, Hereford for example, the bank had a flat-topped profile, with timber and then a stone-fronted rampart in front and a rearward revetment of turf and later stone.

The possible circuit of natural features, along with some planned construction work, enclosed a diamond-shaped area of about 17ha (42 acres). It is possible that a planned street system within the defences may have developed in the Anglo-Saxon period as the High Street, Hailes Street and Chandos Street all run parallel to the long axis of the defences, while North Street, Cowl Street and Malthouse Lane are set at right angles to it. The Mercian palace is said to have stood at the eastern end of Abbey Terrace, immediately to the south of the monastic house, while the Saxon mint may have stood on Hailes Street, although at present there is no firm evidence to support either location. From *c.*1007 Winchcombe lay at the centre of its own shire – Winchcombeshire – which is thought to have incorporated into Gloucestershire in AD 1017.

Benedictine monks were first installed at Winchcombe Abbey in 969, and by the reign of Edward the Confessor (1042–66) the foundation had become one of the foremost houses in England. There is nothing to see today, but the site of the abbey church was excavated during the late nineteenth century when it was found to have stood immediately to the east of the parish church. The cloister and associated monastic buildings stood immediately to the north of the church, and further north still were the abbey fishponds, outbuildings, workshops and gardens, including those of the abbot.

The church of St Peter is thought to have been standing by the eleventh century, so both it and the abbey church were in close proximity. In 1246 Henry de Campden, vicar of Winchcombe, enlarged the chancel and south aisle of the parish church, but by the mid-fifteenth century St Peter's is thought to have become very dilapidated as the townsfolk had begun to worship in the nave of the abbey church. In an attempt to discourage them, Abbot William restored the chancel of St Peter's, hoping that this would provide the inhabitants with an incentive to restore the rest of the fabric. Unfortunately, his beneficence proved to be the downfall of the abbey, for after the Dissolution of the Monasteries between 1536 and 1541 the people of Winchcombe pre-ferred to retain their own parish church.

During or before the reign of Henry II (1154–89) there is believed to have been a castle at Winchcombe; however it is now difficult to locate its site with any certainty, although it is thought to have stood in the area immediately to the south of the parish church. It has been assumed that the medieval market was held in the High Street that formed part of the principal route through the town, along which most travellers would have passed, and that a horse market was held in North Street which was also known as Horse Fair Street. The curved area enclosed by Chandos Street and Bull Lane may indicate the site of an early market which developed outside the entrance to the abbey, and which became in-filled over time.

There are just three interesting medieval buildings in the town: the late fifteenth-century George Hotel was evidently built as a hostel for pilgrims, as the doorway has carved in its spandrels the initials of Abbot Richard Kidderminster and the Old Corner Cupboard Inn is probably sixteenth century, as is the Old White Lion Inn in North Street. There are also Tudor houses with exposed timber framing and overhanging first floors along Hailes Street.

There is little evidence for growth or expansion during much of the post-medieval period, and it was only during the nineteenth century that the settlement developed beyond the bounds of the Anglo-Saxon defences. The period also saw the addition of public buildings such as the town hall (1853) and the Sudeley Almshouses (1865). It was at this time that Abbey Terrace was widened to form the large open area to the south of the site of the abbey.

SUDELEY CASTLE (SP 031276)

The story of Sudeley Castle begins with the large numbers of prehistoric flints found on the estate. During the late Saxon and early Norman periods there appears to have been a village on the site of the later castle. Domesday Book of 1086 records that there were twenty families and fourteen slaves living in the settlement. Tax records of 1175 identify a chapel and a manor house on the site. By 1326 sixteen people were paying tax, which suggests a growing population of about forty families. As in the case of many rural settlements throughout England, the Black Death took its toll on village populations and a tax record of 1381 indicates that perhaps only twenty families survived, ater which the settlement fades from history. It is possible also that Sudeley was the site of a Norman castle dating from the reign of Stephen, but any evidence must lie below the present standing structure. (See plate 5.)

Sir Ralph Boteler (1396–1473), Lord Sudeley, was responsible for building the present structure in about 1441 and this is a possible solution for the disappearance of the village. The castle was crenellated (had walled defences added) in 1458 without a licence from the king, and Boteler was forced to sell it to Edward IV in 1469. The fifteenth-century castle probably consisted of two courtyards surrounded by a moat, with the ornate suite on the east side of the building being the work of Richard, Earl of Gloucestershire (1469–78). Much of the evidence for this edifice was destroyed in the nineteenth century. The castle was extensively altered and added to during the sixteenth century, it being the last home of Katherine Parr, Henry VIII's widow. The structure suffered severely in the Civil War, being slighted in 1649, and it was later neglected and used for building material until the nineteenth century, when major restorations and additions were carried out first in 1837–40 and again in 1863–89. There were lesser improvements in 1901–07 and again in the 1930s, while extensive modernisation to the interior and parts of the exterior has been carried out by the present family living there. The earthwork remains of a sixteenth-century garden (once thought to be the remains of the deserted medieval village) are visible on aerial photographs, with the remains of a parterres, a raised walkway ending at a prospect mound and a dam to create a lake surviving as low earthworks.

The most recent phase of Sudeley Castle's history was as the site of Second World War Prisoner of War Camp 37. It was classed as a purpose-built, standard-type installation. Common buildings and facilities included water towers, offices, officers' mess, a canteen, guard rooms, barrack huts, ablution blocks, cell blocks, a camp reception station (medical facility/hospital), a cookhouse, dining rooms, recreation rooms and living huts or tents. It operated as a German work camp and Italian prisoners were also held here. None of these structures remain.

SECOND WORLD WAR PILLBOX (SP 019 273)

Hidden in a hedge on the right side of the trail near the cricket field is a hexagonal pillbox with all-round vision. It was the most common design, Type 24, with eight loopholes and anti-ricochet wall inside. Built in local stone, it doesn't seem to be a strategic position in relationship to the landscape or the town of Winchcombe, so perhaps it was located to protect the POW camp at Sudeley.

THE BEESMOOR BROOK

This lush valley was used extensively during the Roman period, with a number of high-status buildings having been located along the spring line. The Wadfield Roman villa (SP 023 260) was first discovered in 1863 and lies just west of the Cotswold Way. It was a courtyard villa of three wings, with a bath suite in the south range, living accommodation on the west range and rooms of uncertain function on the north range. A mosaic, badly restored in the late nineteenth century, is beneath a wooden shed in a small copse. The Spoonley Wood Roman villa (SP 049 258) was discovered and excavated in 1882 at the invitation of Mrs Dent, the owner of Sudeley Castle, by the Rev W. Bazeley and Prof J.H. Middleton. It is in a valley-bottom site occupying a spit of ground which slopes very gently westwards, with pleasing views towards what is now Winchcombe. It measured a substantial 52m (170ft) by 58m (190ft) and the plan of the site shows buildings made from local stone, on three sides of a courtyard, with a bath suite on the south, living quarters on the east and its main reception room in the centre opposite an entrance. Outside the courtyard to the west lies an aisled building. Victorian attitudes towards archaeology can be summed up in the visit of the Bristol and Gloucestershire Archaeological Society in 1889, when the Rev Bazeley suggested that it would be valuable for further excavations to take place. Mrs Dent replied 'she would be delighted if the members came, each with a spade, to continue the excavation; if they did so she would provide the bread and cheese'! Rich mosaics recovered from the villa were taken to Sudeley Castle, but their whereabouts are not now known. The walls were partially rebuilt, up to 1.8m (6ft) high in places on the east and south, and a reconstructed mosaic pavement, formerly covered by a wooden shed, is now exposed to weathering following the collapse of the roof. Although the Ordnance Survey map shows a complete outline, the villa is now heavily overgrown and dangerously marshy, even the modern reproductions of the mosaics are suffering from pilfering. On the opposite side of the valley, above the Winchcombe to Guiting Power road at Dunn's Hill, trenching for an oil pipeline revealed an Iron Age structure and the substantial footings of a fourth-century Roman structure with evidence of a mosaic. Mosaic *tesserae* have also been recovered from Lane's Barn (SP 038 268), and Sudeley Lodge (SP 040 270).

In the medieval period the whole valley is likely to have been wooded, the last remnants possibly being Spoonley Wood. Domesday Book records six mills in the area, some of which may have been on the Beesmore Brook, as well as in the Isbourne valley, where there was a tradition of milling up until the nineteenth century and mill ponds and a paper mill remain today.

SECTION 2

STONE
WINCHCOMBE TO PAINSWICK BEACON

The gnawed landscape of Cleeve Common, Charlton Kings Common, Leckhampton and Crickley Hills, which form this section of the route, has produced some spectacular industrial archaeology that has gouged out parts of the earlier sites. The geology of the area is complex but the rocks that interested the quarry owners were all in the Inferior Oolite that rested on the older Liassic clays. At the base of the Inferior Oolite were the Pea Grits: a rock composed of oval bodies about the size of a pea and used largely for troughs, steps, paving and gateposts, as well as being crushed for road stone. Above that were the Lower and Upper limestones, which could be 'freely' removed from the rock in neatly rectangular sections valuable for the facing of walls of large buildings. Above these massive limestones were the ragstones, closely bedded limestones the blocks of which were only one or two feet apart. A simplified way of looking at the uses of these limestones is that the ragstones were used for the drystone walling seen along the route and for buildings that were of the medieval period (or echoing it as nineteenth-century Neo-Gothic architecture), whereas the freestones were used for classical buildings copying Greek and Roman styles, to be found especially in Cheltenham.

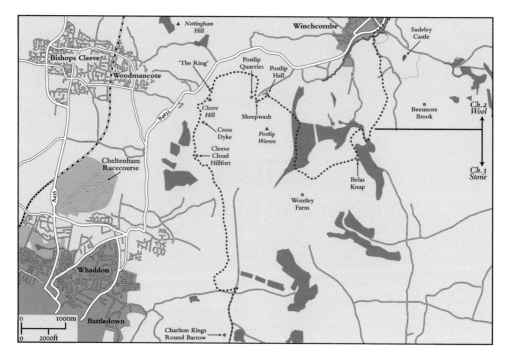

Stone: Winchcombe to Cleeve Cloud hill fort.

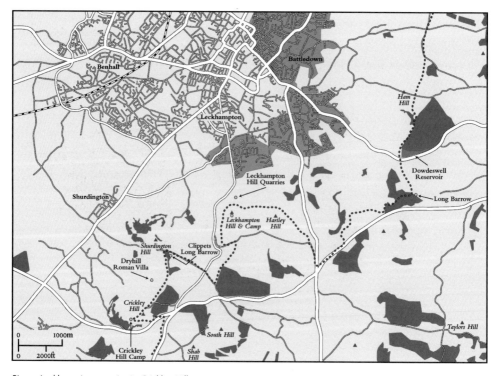

Stone: Leckhampton quarries to Crickley Hill.

BELAS KNAP (SP 021 254)

The barrow acts as a pivot for the 360-degree view seen from every part of plateau of Cleeve Common; in wintertime, when the leaves have dropped off the oaks and beeches of the plantation to the east, it is possible to see the bowl-shaped valley of the Beesmore Brook below, and beyond it the high ground of the Cotswold escarpment to the north. This is not to say that the sites within the vista were part of a territory, but people within the area would certainly have been aware of Belas Knap. (See plate 6.)

Belas Knap is a 'lateral' Neolithic chambered long barrow consisting of a mound, trapezoidal in plan, and orientated north–south, constructed primarily of Oolitic slabs. It is about 55m (178ft) in length, roughly 20m (60ft) at its widest and between 3m and 4m (13ft) tall. At the northern end of the mound is a fore-court, flanked by two projections roughly composed of drystone walling in the shape of a funnel leading the eye to a 'false entrance' consisting of two standing stones and a lintel stone. Four burial chambers burrow into the mound: two on the east side, one at the southern end and another on the west side of the barrow. The chambers were originally roofed with slabs of Oolitic limestone.

The photogenic, serene and peaceful grass-covered mound and neat stone chambers owe much of their present character to a programme of restora-tion carried out by the Ministry of Works in the late 1920s. Before this a very different scene would have greeted visitors – a ruined and desolate site bat-tered and scarred by investigations in the 1860s. In the spring of 1863 Joseph Chamberlayne, the owner of the monument, and Lauriston Winterbotham,

15 Belas Knap in 1913 before unsympathetic 'restoration'. *Edward J. Burrow, 'Ancient Entrenchments and Camps of Gloucestershire', 1924, p. 12*

16 Belas Knap from the west. *Author's collection*

a Cheltenham doctor, commenced a series of excavations on the mound. Lifting a large slab near the south-east corner, the excavators revealed a chamber with the partial remains of four human skeletons, including two complete skulls. With their archaeological appetite whetted, they then undertook a more ambitious excavation at the northern end leading to the discovery of the magnificent drystone-walled face of the barrow and its stone portal. On further investigation this proved not to be the entrance to a chamber but rather a megalithic construction built, perhaps as a kind of ritual arena, in front of the mound. The removal of the great horizontal 'lintel' stone above the portal revealed the remains of five young children and an adult skull.

News of the discoveries reached Walter Lawrence, a local landowner and archaeologist, and he joined the excavation team on site the following year, when they drove a trench around much of the barrow to reveal two opposing side chambers. The eastern chamber contained the remains of twelve skeletons found in a 'squatting' position on a stone-flagged floor, while the chamber on the west contained the remains of fourteen skeletons. In the following June the excavation was completed with the digging of a trench from behind the portal towards the centre of the tomb, which was met by a trench cut from one side chamber to the other. In the process, the excavators revealed a circle of stones amongst a mass of ashes beneath the mound and between the north-west and north-east chambers. Lawrence described this as the remains of an 'Altar of Sacrifice or Worship, and used at some time for Druidical rites'. Altogether, the excavations of the chambers and portal produced the remains of some thirty-eight people of differing ages and both sexes. Typically for the time, this strange group was interpreted by the excavators as being the victims of human sacrifice.

In common with many nineteenth-century excavators, those at Belas Knap were perplexed by the state of the burial chambers. They found fragments from many individuals jumbled together, leading to the suggestion that the remains had been disturbed at a later date. But throughout the 1860s and '70s evidence was mounting from sealed chambers elsewhere to suggest that the discoveries at Belas Knap were not unique. Archaeologists began to see that the burial rite used in 'Cotswold-Severn' Neolithic tombs, such as Belas Knap, was not that of complete, articulated skeletons seen in inhumations from other periods, but was something altogether different. The many theories advanced for this Neolithic burial rite – including cannibalism and ritual slaughter – were eventually narrowed down to just two: first, that tombs acted as ossuaries, where de-fleshed bones were placed or stacked in the chambers; and second, that successive interments were made where corpses were deposited and then dragged away at a later date to be replaced by an in-comer.

One of the visitors to the Belas Knap excavations of 1863 was John Thurnam, the medical superintendent of the Wiltshire County Asylum, who had a long involvement with archaeology and craniology – the study of skulls. Thurnam had examined many prehistoric crania from barrow sites and he was sent seventeen skulls from Belas Knap to analyse, the largest group yet seen from a chambered long barrow. Craniologists of the time used a ratio based on length and width measurements, known as the cranial index, to divide skulls into two basic types: 'dolichocephalic', long and narrow in shape, and 'brachycephalic', broad and round in shape. Based on his observations at sites like Belas Knap, Thurnam established his famous axiom, 'long barrows, long skulls; round barrows, round skulls'. The long skulls were found in long barrows and never in association with metallic artefacts, while round skulls were found in round barrows, sometimes with metalwork – but the single adult skull from the portal was clearly not long headed, and was decidedly round. Thurnam tentatively suggested that it represented a secondary or later burial; but the excavators believed this to be impossible and both parties settled on the idea that the round skull belonged to a man from a different tribe to the builders of the long barrow, who had been sacrificed in honour of those buried in the chambers.

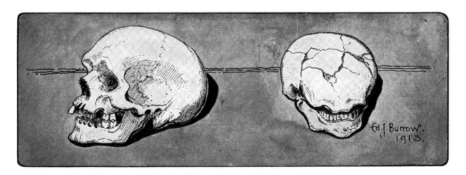

17. The long and narrow shaped 'dolichocephalic' skulls were deemed 'feebler in development' and characteristic of the Welsh peoples. The broad and round 'brachycephalic' skulls were equated with the Scandinavian invaders with more favourably conditioned brains. *Edward J. Burrow, 'Ancient Entrenchments and Camps of Gloucestershire', 1924, p. 11*

In the footsteps of Thurnam came George Rolleston, a professor of anatomy at Oxford. In 1877, he expounded his theories on British prehistoric peoples in the book *British Barrows*, written jointly with the famous barrow opener William Greenwell. Basing his statements on evidence from Gloucestershire long barrows such as Belas Knap, Rolleston believed the narrow-headed race to be weak and short in stature, with poor brain development. He suggested that remnants of this race could still be seen among the Welsh and inhabitants of western Britain, being 'the black-haired type ... feebler in development ... and larger in skull form'. In Rolleston's version of prehistory, this race was swept away by the taller, stronger, broad-headed people with 'more favourably conditioned brains' who came as conquerors from Scandinavia.

Thurnam's and Rolleston's racist theories gained considerable credibility in the late Victorian period and survived well into the earlier twentieth century. The considerable moral repugnance felt towards Victorian anthropology and its role in the rise of fascist ideology in the 1930s caused the argument over long and round skulls to be sidelined and eventually dismissed. Instead an archaeological culture based on shared, social characteristics and material culture rather than race or biological type became dominant. The identification of the Bronze Age incomers based on their material culture, including metalwork and Beaker pottery vessels, became a more acceptable alternative.

Clearly, the long barrow was as compelling in the Bronze Age as now, and a round barrow was placed 70m (229ft) to the south west at (SP 020 253). The barrow has been largely ploughed out, but it can still be seen as a low rise if seen against the horizon. The area between the long and round barrows is no longer ploughed, preserving the respectful relationship.

WONTLEY FARM (SP 008 247)

Wontley Farm is in a steep but shallow valley on the site of a deserted medieval village. The small hamlet was known as Huntlowe in the medieval period and later as Wontley, but had disappeared by the sixteenth century. The valued protection accorded by this valley in a windswept upland is demonstrated by a concentration of flints, chiefly flakes and a scatter of Romano-British pottery, mainly of second to fourth centuries, found at Wontley. Be warned: although the ruined farm buildings look attractive as shade or for exploration, you will be sharing them with a large colony of adders!

THE VALLEY OF THE RIVER ISBOURNE

Postlip Mills (SP 008 270)

The River Isbourne and its tributary, Beesmoor Brook, are the only two watercourses along the northern end of the Cotswold Way that are deep enough and have steep enough profiles to produce a head of water capable of driving mill wheels. The lack of iron in the Isbourne Brook also made it highly suitable for papermaking, and mills were strung out along its 21km (13 miles) to Evesham, where it joined the River Avon. While we do not know how many mills were along the Beesmore Brook, three are known on the Isbourne between Postlip House and Winchcombe. Domesday Book of 1086 records a flour mill with a large waterwheel owned by the Abbot of Winchcombe and used for grinding corn until at least 1663. Between 1782 and 1795 the Postlip Mill produced corn and also paper, which was made from rags beaten to pulp by machinery driven by power from waterwheels and, after 1852, by steam. A walk down the usually muddy and slippery footpath to the right of the gateway of Postlip Hall skirts one of the millponds, which has recently been altered to provide a recreation area for the residents. With the invention of the ballpoint pen, blotting paper has become increasingly redundant. However, the making of paper continues at Postlip Mill, with the specialist products being used for filtering air, in face masks and in vacuum cleaners, as well as for beer making and wine filtration.

Postlip Hall (SO 998 268)

The earliest part of the Hall (or House) appears to be the east wing, which is of two storeys with a range of mullioned windows; to this was added the large south wing. It dates from the sixteenth century or early seventeenth century and is built around an inner courtyard.

18 Postlip Hall. *Author's collection*

The Watery Bottom Sheepwash (SO 997 265)

The sheepwash is on the spring line, where water percolating through the lower freestone meets the Upper Lias clay and comes to the surface as the headwater of the River Isbourne. It was constructed in 1896 when drawings show that a dam was made across the stream to create a source of water to feed the sheep wash below. The circular sheep wash itself is stone-lined, and c.2.5m (8.2ft) in diameter, with an escape ramp for the animals. The site is one

of the last sheep washes to be built in Gloucestershire, and was still in use until at least the mid-1930s. It was repaired in 1994.

19 The sheep dip at Watery Bottom – note the stairs for sheep access. *Author's collection*

Postlip Freestone Quarries (SO 995 265)

These quarries were rented out by the Abbot of Winchcombe in the Middle Ages and then by successive lords of the manor and continued to be worked with various degrees of success right through to the twentieth century, resulting in the scarred, broken and rugged landscape we see today. A 40m (132ft) thickness of freestone on a lower and upper terrace has produced large tips of waste material. Some of the tips may indicate mines, as even the cheap roadstone could have been excavated underground. Stone from these quarries was certainly used at Hailes, Tewkesbury and Winchcombe Abbeys, and also the 'Rotunda' in Montpellier in Cheltenham. (See plate 7.)

20 Quarries and trackways at Postlip. *Author's collection*

Settlement (SO 986 269)

As you pass through the gate with the golf course on your left, above the second green in the 'rough' are the remains of some un-dated ditch enclosures which are roughly rectangular, covering about 0.6ha (1.5 acres). The ditches are up to 6m (20ft) across and 1.2m (4ft) deep. There may well have been many more settlements sited along the flanks of the hill that have been removed by quarrying. At King's Beeches (SO 982 267) pits were found in the quarry edge with fourth-century coins, poorly made pottery and a variety of stone slabs. Human and animal bones were also found. The original excavators in 1904 (both geologists) suggested an early Iron Age date. Both of these sites might be related to the Ring.

The Ring (SO 984 266)

This unusual ringwork possibly represents an Iron Age or Roman homestead enclosure, defined by a ditch and an inner and/or outer bank on a moderate west-facing slope. It is certainly not defensive and its situation on such a slight slope has necessitated an external ditch 1m (3.3ft) deep on the upper side with an internal bank 0.5m (1.6ft) high, while on the lower side the bank is external and the ditch internal. The enclosure ditch measures *c* 2.5m (8ft) wide and is flanked internally by a bank measuring up to 5m (16ft) wide. The ditch encloses an area measuring 56m (183m) long by 48m (157ft) wide at its widest points, and is orientated south-west to north-east. An entrance is situated to the south-west. A level area in the enclosure's centre, in its present form, is probably part of a golf course, and inside the entrance, on the south, is a likely hut platform.

Immediately north-east of the Ring (SO 985 266) and similarly plannned, though on a smaller scale, is a scooped, platformed ring-work about 2m (6.5ft) deep on a slight north-west slope. The entrance on the south-west appears to be original and, although undated, it is probably an Iron Age or Roman hut, with a flat interior about 9.1m (30 ft) across.

NOTTINGHAM HILL CAMP (CENTRED ON SO 987 282)

Across the main road between Cheltenham and Winchcombe is Nottingham Hill Camp. This multi-phase site on the spur of the main escarpment comprises a Bronze Age barrow cemetery and the site of a Bronze Age hoard, as well as an Iron Age promontory hill fort. There is also coin evidence for Roman occupation and documentary suggestions of early medieval occupation. The feature is cut off the main escarpment and is flanked on either side

21 Nottingham Hill Camp. *Edward J. Burrow, 'Ancient Entrenchments and Camps of Gloucestershire',*
1924, p. 95

by a linear ditch enclosing some 45.8ha (120 acres). The south-western end
of these features may have been damaged by quarrying and the north-eastern
end is obscured by tree cover. It is likely that the steep slopes have been aug-
mented by scarping. Iron Age coffins and coins and also Roman coins are
reported from the encampment, but all finds have been lost. Two Bronze Age
swords were ploughed up in 1972 and a subsequent excavation, following a
proton magnetometer and metal detection survey, revealed an undisturbed
late Bronze Age hoard contained possibly in a box structure. It consisted of
three leaf-shaped swords, a looped palstave, a socketed knife, a bronze cylinder, cast conical-headed rivets, cast bronze rings with bronze strap work,
a tanged chisel, a tanged 'awl', a whetstone and a casting jet (a plug of metal
which is knocked out after an artefact is cast and fits exactly into the opening of a mould). The deposition of the hoard within the hill fort could be
entirely fortuitous and there may have been centuries between the events.
Other features recorded were a markedly worn 'track' running north-west to
south-east, hearth remains in the middle of the track alignment, five sub-cir-
cular soil-filled features on either side of the track and *c.*150 pottery sherds. It is
possible that the soil-filled features were actually made by tractor. A Neolithic
discoidal flint scraper was found in proximity to the hearth. Surface collections have been made over the entire internal area of Nottingham Hill Camp,
but no significant levels of occupational debris were detected. Finds consisted
of occasional flint-working debris, gritstone fragments, and pebble fragments
with heat cracking and abrasion marks.

RIFLE FIRING RANGE (CENTRED ON SO 987 269)

A possible twentieth-century small-arms or rifle-firing range is visible as earthworks on aerial photographs. The site extends over an area that measures 80m (262ft) long by nearly 60m (197ft) wide. It comprises two parallel linear ditches measuring *c*.4m (13ft) wide that are situated 65m (213ft) apart, each of which is flanked on both sides by linear banks measuring up to 5m (16ft) wide. The site is orientated roughly north-east/south-west, although the ditches and banks are orientated roughly north-west/south-east.

The northernmost ditch measures 4m (13ft) wide and 57m (187ft) long and may have been used as the 'butts'. The shorter south-eastern ditch and flanking banks between may have acted as the firing line. (See plate 8.)

CLEEVE HILL AND COMMON (CENTRED ON SO 990 260)

Cleeve Hill Common forms the highest point of the Cotswolds and as it has never been ploughed, the archaeological earthworks have tended to endure. However, there are a number of problems with their survival and in ascertaining individual ages. The Common has been eaten into at many places by, largely, post-medieval quarrying, and this is particularly obvious on the escarpment along which the Cotswold Way runs. In 1818 the Common was the site of the first Cheltenham racecourse and some levelling had to take place to make a more even surface. In 1891 a golf course was set out and throughout its existence it has changed configuration a number of times, leaving the remains of tees, bunkers and greens, which, frustratingly, have some of the same characteristics as much earlier monuments, such as house platforms and barrows. A

22 Cleeve Edge: the quarries are exploiting the Upper Freestones of the Inferior Oolite system. *Author's collection*

large number of trackways extend across Cleeve Common and are visible on aerial photographs as earthworks. They represent the collective result of centuries of routeways across the common, potentially from later prehistory onwards. Many of the tracks are visible as combinations of two parallel ditches (indicating wheeled vehicles) and can be associated with the large number of quarries.

At Cleeve Common the limestones are at their greatest thickness and variety, and there is a corresponding diversity of quarries. The 'Roman Camp Quarry' provided Pea Grit until 1910 and it was used in much medieval church work north of Gloucester, in particular for steps, gravestones and coffins. It provided stone for Cheltenham Town Hall in 1901, although Bath stone was most commonly used for the exterior. Castle Quarry was used until a few years later and the remains of winding gear for the quarries can be seen in the spoil below Castle Rock, which is now used for rock climbing.

An advert in the 1914 *Kelly's Directory* placed by Arthur Yield boasts that the 'stone from Cleeve Hill was used in the Cheltenham College Chapel, the Great Western Station and most of the public buildings in Cheltenham and the County of Gloucestershire and adjoining Counties. Recent work supplied; the restoration of Magdalen College, Oxford, the Restoration of Romsey Abbey near Southampton, the Restoration of Tewkesbury Abbey' and other similar buildings.

The stone was also used for building houses as well as field walls and surfacing roads.

An early Bronze Age axe and a single-edged knife have been found on the Common, as have two miniature bronze implements, possibly votive;

the finds suggest a temple site. The larger one, which takes the form of a tanged dagger, is 7cm (2.75in) long and of wafer thickness throughout. The other, resembling a socketed ploughshare, is 4cm (1.5in) long with a maximum thickness of 1mm (0.03in). Unfortunately, we have no idea where they were found.

23 Winding gear below Castle Rock at Cleeve Hill. *Author's collection*

CROSS DYKE (SO 983 263 TO SO 989264)

An undated dyke, probably from the Iron Age, extends for over 0.48km (0.3 miles) across the ridge of Cleeve Hill. Much of the dyke comprises a bank some 4.6m (15ft) wide standing up to 0.9m (3ft) high above a ditch of similar width. The dyke's form changes over its length and the differing methods of construction suggest more than one phase of construction. The western 200m (656ft) is a ditch averaging 1m (3.2ft) deep with a bank up to 0.7m (2.2ft) high on each side. The central 200m (656ft) has a more V-shaped ditch with a single bank on the south or downhill side. The eastern 200m (656ft) is a slightly hollowed terrace with a slope 0.7m high (2.2ft) on the south side of the terrace. As the dyke has no obvious original entrance, although it is broken by several tracks, the feature might possibly be a land division.

CLEEVE CLOUD HILL FORT (SO 984 254)

The Iron Age fort is bivallate with an intermediate berm, now enclosing about 1.2ha (3 acres) of ground sloping gently west to the partly quarried cliff edge. No original entrance survives. The banks and ditches have been disturbed in places by quarrying, and on the north the outer defences have been cut through to make a golf course. A rectangular platform abutting the inner bank 30.5m (100ft) from its north end is probably recent. Each bank and each ditch is about 9m (30ft) across, the banks standing 2.4m (8.5ft) to 3.3m (11ft) above the ditches. The berm, which separates the inner ditch from the outer bank, is 9m (30ft) wide in a disturbed area south of the golf green; elsewhere it is half this width or less. Witts points out that the situation of the fortress is 'remarkable, inasmuch as the ground rises from above the level of the camp to the east, but there seems to have been watchtowers

24 Cleeve Cloud Camp: note how it is overlooked by higher ground. *Edward J. Burrow, 'Ancient Entrenchments and Camps of Gloucestershire', 1924, p. 61*

SECTION 2

on the summit of the hill, traces of which can still be seen'. No trace remains of these features today, and it is unlikely that they ever existed, but the single, rather tortured and stunted beech tree is probably the last remaining example of a plantation set out before 1919.

A banked circle on the cliff edge inside the fort, and another 45.7m (150ft) outside to the north, are both about 15.2m (50ft) in diameter. Witts refers to another and smaller ring outside the hill fort; all three were assumed to represent buildings attached to the 'camp'. Each of these features are probably of recent date, perhaps tree rings similar to the one surrounding the 'Three Maidens' just in front of the rampart to the south.

Garrett, in his *From a Cotswold Height: A Description of Country Scenes in Gloucestershire* (1919, pp. 62–3), recalls a field trip by the Cotteswold Field Club on 10 July 1917 where, after visiting Cheltenham Museum to examine human remains, they sat down on the turf to eat lunch at the 'Roman Camp', while one member (probably Garrett himself) delivered a broad, descriptive address on Cleeve Common and its surroundings (I always imagine him pointing to the top of Nottingham Hill). Then it was the turn of the President, W St Clair Baddeley:

> tall, bearded and very learned in archaeological studies, pursued at home and abroad, distinguished among local authorities, takes up the subject allotted to him and speaks of the, mis-called Roman camps which cap prominent parts of the Cotswold Escarpment from end to end, as well as the outliers … The speaker also makes a score of little excursions into subjects that have little relation to the camps but which, out of his archaeological erudition, very neatly and interestingly creep into his discourse.

THE VIEW FROM THE CLEEVE HILL ESCARPMENT (SP 983 260)

The Severn floodplain is made up of heavy clay soils topped with alluvium, making archaeological sites difficult to find because of the lack of the formation of crop marks – even intensive field walking does not pick up substantial settlements. It was rescue archaeology in advance of the M5 motorway's construction that indicated a significant density of settlement of the late Iron Age, Roman and medieval periods in the Severn Vale. However, since 1991 archaeological fieldwork and excavations before domestic and industrial development have transformed our view of this low-lying area. The Wormington to Tirley pipeline demonstrated the 'double-edged sword' of contract archaeology. A thin, snaking slice of only 4–6 metres (13–19.5 feet) was available for excavation, though when sites were discovered the area was extended. However, this arbitrary line through a highly populated landscape did give insights into the density of settlements and different methods of locating sites were trialled. The resulting evidence demonstrated an intensively exploited landscape with basic farmsteads practising mixed farming; pasture being the most dominant form of agriculture.

Fan gravels and sands at the base of the escarpment were created from the deposition of large amounts of fractured Jurassic limestone from the Cotswolds during the last glaciations. They probably formed a continuous sheet across the Severn Valley, but have been dissected and diminished by the Severn's braided watercourses. These fan-gravel spreads in the Severn Valley were intensively used for settlement and this is seen on the outskirts of Tewkesbury around the base of Bredon Hill, and at Bishop's Cleeve, directly below you. As you can see, the village has developed recently, with large housing estates and supermarkets which have offered an opportunity to explore the sequential occupation of the locality.

There is considerable evidence of a late Iron Age agricultural settlement focused on the production of food, such as growing and processing of grain and other cereals. Evidence for small-scale craft industries such as bone working and iron smithing has also been found. Boundary ditches interpreted as being used for livestock management, dominated by cattle, sheep and goats, suggest an overall mixed economy. The centre of the late Iron Age settlement has not yet been identified, but continuity of settlement into the Roman period is indicated by Iron Age ditches being re-cut, although the evidence also demonstrates that the community moved westward in the late first century. Materials found on some of the sites from this period indicate that a villa or small agricultural settlement lay close by, but the Roman masonry structures remain elusive – although a possible hypocaust, the presence of *opus signinum* floors made of crushed tile, *tessarae* from mosaics, and wall plaster indicate a well-appointed structure, possibly a villa dated to the third and fourth centuries. The botanical evidence suggests that in the Roman period oats, wheat and barley were grown. Evidence from boundary ditches also indicates that livestock management was dominated by cattle and sheep, the carcasses being butchered and processed for consumption and some by-products. An extensive system of agricultural enclosures suggests discrete zones for horticulture, small-scale industrial activity to meet the needs of the settlement and leather tanning or flax retting. It has been estimated that this settlement may have covered about 3.8ha (9.5 acres) and survived in some form until the fourth century. These landscape conditions exist along the base of the Cotswold escarpment and there are probably a number of other settlements of this age yet to be discovered.

The above-ground archaeology across the Vale is particularly concerned with the spirituality, power and politics of the medieval church. Except for a small section in the Bath and Wells diocese from North Stoke to Bath, the Cotswold Way is in the medieval diocese of Worcester, the cathedral being hidden behind Bredon Hill. You will see two medieval abbeys in the distance: Tewkesbury, whose patron saint was the Blessed Virgin Mary, and St Peter's Abbey in Gloucester (later to become the cathedral after the Dissolution of the Monasteries). Winchcombe housed the now completely destroyed abbey of St Kenelm. Each of these centres of spiritual and political power pin down the medieval religious landscape with a mesh of parishes, covering all of the available land. The church may be a symbol of spiritual power, but there are also indications of temporal power in that Bishop's Cleeve was the manor of the Bishop of Worcester and Prestbury, just out of sight, belonged to the Bishop of Hereford, whose moated palace was excavated in 1951. Llanthony Abbey of Gloucester also had lands in that village. As we have seen, each of these religious entities owned much land in the Cotswolds.

The early Church also played a significant role in the development of towns. From the seventh century onwards minsters were founded to serve as centres for the conversion and administration of large areas of England, and Bishop's Cleeve was the site of one of these. A minster usually consisted of a church and outbuildings within an enclosure, served by a priest and a number of monastic or secular assistants. Such concentrations of priests would have required goods and services, which would in turn have attracted secular settlement to the area to serve those needs, and it is possible that these complexes may have provided the closest equivalent to towns in England until the creation of the burhs in the ninth century.

You can see much ridge and furrow and the oddly shaped, small fields suggest early enclosures, with the fossilised 'S' and 'C' shapes being apparent in some of their hedges. Much of the rest of the landscape has the right-angled fields characteristic of the Enclosure Movement, their rectangularity making the surveyor's job easier.

Huddlestone's Table (SO 984 253)

Immediately below the Cleeve Cloud hill fort is a cubical block of stone measuring 0.9m (3ft) by 0.9m (3ft) by 0.5m (1.6ft) and marked on the Ordnance Survey map as Huddlestone's Table. It is said to have been set in position about 300 years ago by the Delaberes of Southam, being a facsimile of an ancient stone formerly existing there. According to local lore it marks the spot to which King Kenulph of Mercia escorted his guests after the dedication of Winchcombe Abbey c.AD 798.

Northfield Round Barrow (SO 990 216)

This round barrow is now 1.5m (4ft) high and only 10m (32ft) or so in diameter, and close to the hedge of a field running parallel to the Cotswold Way. In 1912, at the time of its excavation by S.W. Billings, it was apparently 30.5m (100ft) in circumference and 3.6m (12ft) in height. Hill, describing these excavations for the first time in 1930, states that the mound had been built up by alternate layers of stone and earth, possibly stabilised by the erection of four huge slabs near its centre. He makes the perceptive comment that the pottery sherds in the rubble may have been part of a ritual activity rather than just being thrown on to the mound with the soil. Within the mound, and extending to almost half its height from ground level, a shaft, or flue, had been constructed. This shaft, sealed by one of the stony layers of the barrow, contained a funeral pyre; 'the ground was black and stodgy'. A 15cm (6in) layer of burnt bones and charcoal at ground level covered numerous bones. Three short cists, thought by Hill to have been those of primary burials, were found in the body of the barrow, on its east side, about 1.8m (6ft) above ground level. They contained the dismembered bones of a man about 1.5m (5ft 10in) tall, whose bones indicated that he was a 'great runner' and a woman and child, each bone wrapped separately in clay. Two bone pins near the man's head indicated some sort of packaging which had not survived. Hill concluded that the woman and child had been killed as an offering at the funeral of the chief with the intent that they should accompany him to the land of future existence. With them were found a flint knife, saw, fabricator, whetstone, crystal and polished white pebble, and again there is the insight that the positioning of these artefacts did not indicate that they had been 'thrown upon the remains as if mechanically observing some tribal custom, but had been carefully laid upon the bones that suggested in a way belief in a future existence'. It is more likely that they were contemporary 'satellite' burials.

Dowdeswell Reservoir and Water Treatment Works (SO 196 198)

The reservoir and water treatment works were built in 1886 by Cheltenham Corporation to supply the town with drinking water, and subsequently became part of the Severn Trent network. Severn Trent closed the water treatment works upon the commissioning of the Mythe Treatment Works on the River Severn, and the reservoir itself became a flood-storage reservoir for the River Chelt in an attempt to protect the town of Cheltenham from flooding from the east. The town nonetheless suffered flooding in July 2007, though this was not only from the River Chelt at Dowdeswell, but from all the streams which run off the limestone scarp to join the Chelt within the town and its outskirts.

Dowdeswell Long Barrow (SO 992 185)

This long barrow is aligned east–west with a large hollow in the centre of the eastern part of the mound caused by the robbing of the barrow for curiosity, or to get at the stone slabs that would have been found in its centre. A more insidious threat is ploughing around the feature, which is gradually encroaching on its flanks. It has been suggested that the original length of the long barrow was 46m (150ft), but by 1960 this had been reduced to 30.5m (100ft), with a width of 14.5m (48ft) and a height of 1.8m (6ft). In 1998 further ploughing along the sides had shrunk the barrow's dimensions to 28.7m (94ft) long and 12m (39ft) wide, with its height remaining at 1.8m (6ft).

Dowdeswell 'The Castles' (SO 998 191)

Reached by a footpath from the Cotswold Way, this is a univallate and unexcavated enclosure, presumably early Iron Age. It has been damaged on all sides by ploughing except for a short length of the south-west side which forms part of the footpath. The enclosure covers c.6ha (14 acres) with a bank 7m (23ft wide), 2.5m (8ft) above a ditch, which is 7.5m (25ft) wide. A considerable amount of Roman pottery has been recovered from the northern half of the enclosure, and with a number of large villas in the locality it would be unusual for a then up-standing enclosure not to be used for some purpose, possibly as a village.

THE LECKHAMPTON HILL QUARRIES (CENTRED ON SO 948 185)

While the Leckhampton Hill quarries were on a larger scale than others in the area, possibly accounting for over half the stone available, the vast majority was not building stone, or it was not suitable for sawing into the shapes needed by 'classical' Cheltenham. It was more suitable for road stone or for building walls or houses. Quarrying on the hill dates back at least four centuries, with the most prolific period between 1797 and 1892, but the quarries were always of prime importance and produced over two million tons of several different rock types between the 1790s and the 1920s.

Stone was transported down steep inclines and worked by gravity, such that a laden tram descending would pull up an empty one and a winding drum fitted with a brake was used to control the operation. The tram roads were probably all 1.07m (3ft 6in) rail gauge and the individual rails were approximately 0.91m (1yrd) long. The rails were plateways with L-section rails (tram-plates) where the vertical flange guided the flangeless wheels of the trams. The first of seven inclines, the Devil's Chimney Incline (B1), was built c.1795 by Charles Brandon Trye, who had recently acquired the

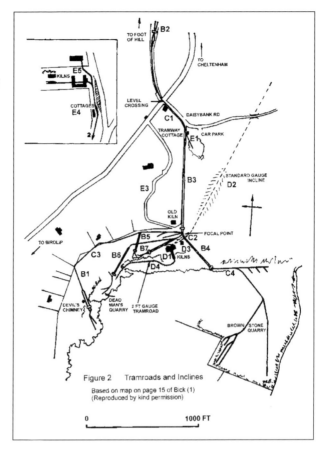

25 Leckhampton quarries, tramways and inclines, based on Bick. *Ray Wilson, 'The Industrial of Leckhampton Hill', GSIA, Volume for 2001, pp. 35–46*

Leckhampton Estate. It is likely that its construction isolated from the cliff face a pillar of rock that was subsequently fashioned into what is known today as the 'Devil's Chimney'.

In 1810 the Bottom (B2) and Middle (B3) Inclines were built to give Trye's new horse-drawn Gloucester and Cheltenham Railway access to Leckhampton Quarries. In the *Gloucester Journal* of 1 July 1816, a Mr Walford, who owned the quarries, advertised:

> an ornamental stone from the newly worked quarries at Leckhampton Hill, which for beauty and durability cannot be excelled. Having an IRON-RAIL-ROAD from the works to the waterside at Gloucester, there may be had there in large dimensions, as well as all building sizes, either, hewn or in the rough on very reasonable terms.

The Top Incline was built in 1830 as an extension to the line formed by the Bottom and Middle Inclines some twenty years earlier. The new incline gave

26 The Devil's Chimney, Leckhampton, partly the result of the laying of an incline for a quarry. *Countryside Agency: Jo Ward*

access to the top of the hill and in particular access to the extensive brownstone quarry on the summit, which worked the ragstones that were used in the building of the Gloucestershire County Shire Hall, begun in 1812. Several of the tramroads and inclines met at SO 949 185.

An ambitious scheme was proposed in 1922, in which four large limekilns (D1) were to be built and the lime produced would be transported off the hill on a standard-gauge railway constructed between 1922 and 1924 to join the Great Western Railway at Charlton Kings.

However, for technical and other reasons the project was not a success; all production stopped about two years later and the plant was sold in August 1927. Today only the concrete bases remain of the four steel limekilns that were erected in 1924 (SO 948 185 – SO 948 185). They were 23.5m (77ft) high and were manufactured by the firm Priest of Middlesborough, and were fired using gas that was made in the kilns from coal. The design was new and did not work very well. It failed to produce lime of a consistent quality. (See plate 11.)

LECKHAMPTON HILL CAMP (CENTRED ON SO 947 183)

Outside the hill fort on the eastern side is an enigmatic feature once thought to be a round barrow. However, several examples of square structures with platforms inside have been found throughout the UK and have been interpreted as late Iron Age temples. If this is the case then it would be expected that inside the banks would be found similar structures to that at West Down, Uley, further along the trail to the south. There the shrine was discovered to contain timber buildings within a large, square, ditched enclosure, and inside that a smaller trapezoidal timber structure. Pits with votive offerings for the deity were found with animal, human and infant bones, as well as high-status pottery and metalwork. (See plates 9 and 10.)

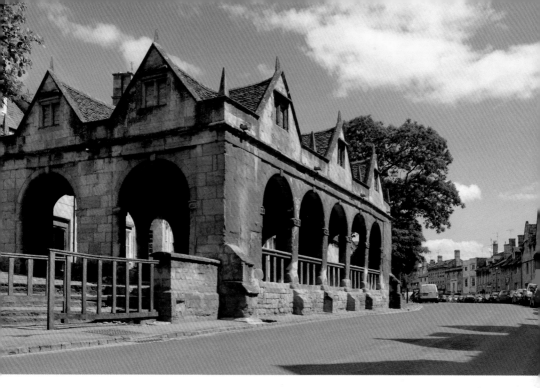

1. Chipping Campden Market Hall, built by Sir Baptist Hicks in the early seventeenth century, possibly on the site of an earlier one. *Countryside Agency: Jo Ward*

2. Royal Observer Corps Monitoring Post at Broadway Tower, built as part of an extensive network designed to confirm and report hostile aircraft and nuclear attacks on the United Kingdom. This site was opened during June 1960 and closed in September 1991. *Author's collection*

3. The Broadway Hotel, one of the few medieval buildings to survive in the small town. *Author's collection*

4. Hailes Abbey, showing the walls of the cloister surviving to full height. *Countryside Agency: Jo Ward*

5. Sudeley Castle, with damage caused during the English Civil War. *The Sudeley Estate*

6. Belas Knap, with its false entrance and horn-work. *Author's collection*

7. Postlip Quarries, the substantial 'tailings' of rubble possibly coming from tunnelling. *Author's collection*

8. Cleeve Hill, below the escarpment. The image contains quarry waste and a golf course, and the parallel lines in the centre left are the possible traces of a Second World War firing range. *Author's collection*

9. Leckhampton Hill, from the south with the hill fort and quarry faces. The dark green circles are natural 'fairy rings' and not archaeological features. *Kite Aerial Photographs courtesy of Hamish Fenton*

10. Leckhampton Hill from the north with the hill fort and the possible square temple enclosure. *Kite Aerial Photographs courtesy of Hamish Fenton*

11. Leckhampton Quarry lime kilns, built in 1922 and closed down two years later. *Author's collection*

12. The 'Birdlip Treasure' and the woman's skull associated with it. *Gloucester City Museum*

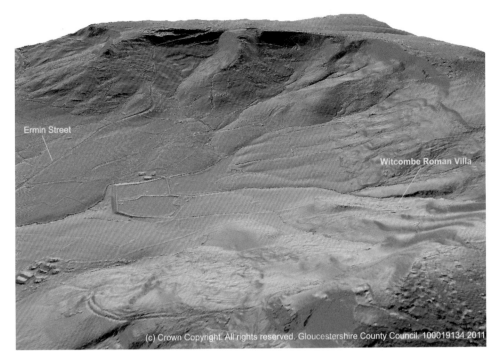

13. A LiDAR image of the embayment between Crickley Hill and Great Witcombe Roman villa, with Ermin Street descending towards Gloucester. The Cotswold Way route follows the skyline. *Gloucestershire County Council and Cranham Local History Society*

14. Great Witcombe Roman Villa and the Cotswold escarpment, demonstrating the visibility of the building. *Cotswold Archaeology*

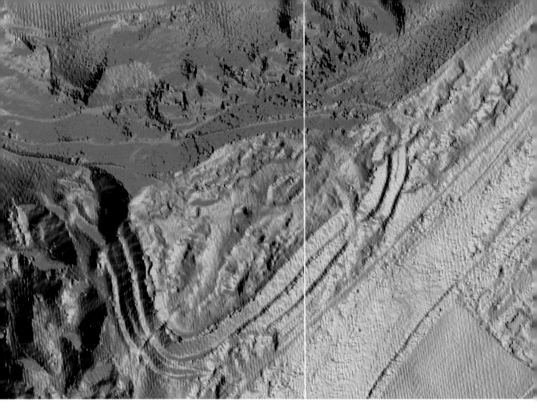

15. A LiDAR image of Painswick Beacon, showing the hill fort and golf tees, bunkers and greens. *Gloucestershire County Council and Cranham Local History Society*

16. The view along the escarpment from Haresfield Beacon towards Cam Long Down. The patch of green in the centre-left distance is the site of the Uley Roman temple. Haresfield Beacon may also have been the site of ritual activity. *Author's collection*

17. The overgrown remains of the Second World War bunker associated with the Standish aircraft decoy. *Author's collection*

18. At Black Down, Somerset is a complete decoy bunker similar to the Standish structure. *Author's collection*

19. The Stroudwater Canal under restoration, with Ebley Mill alongside it. *Photograph copyright of Tom Vivian*

20. The central arcade of double rows of cast-iron Doric columns with a round-arched tracery provided a substantial backbone for Stanley Mill. *Author's collection*

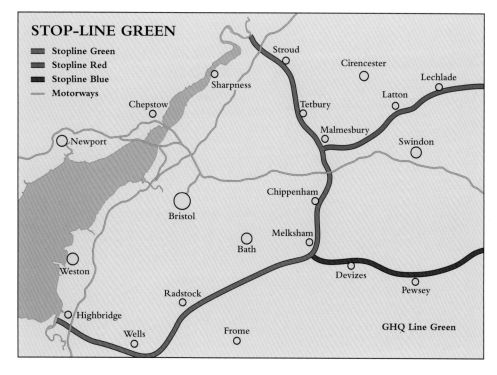

21. The course of the Second World War 'Stop-Line Green' around Bristol and Bath. It uses the Stroudwater Canal as part of the defences. *Alan Strickland*

22. The damage left by early excavation at 'The Toots' on Selsley Common. The long barrow is one of the few along the route not in, or with view obscured by, woodland and demonstrates the visibility of these funerary structures. *Author's collection*

23. The Uley Ritual Complex of Neolithic long barrow at Hetty Pegler's Tump, a possible Bronze Age round barrow, the Roman temple to Mercury and Uley Bury Iron Age hill fort. *Stroud District Museum: Steve Smith*

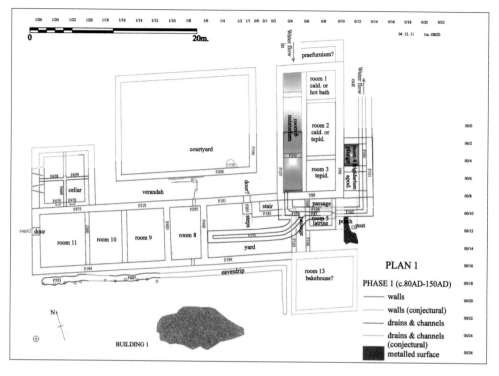

Plan showing grid references along top: 1/26 1/24 1/22 1/20 1/18 1/16 1/14 1/12 1/10 1/8 1/6 1/4 1/2 1/1 0/0 0/1 0/2 0/4 0/6 0/8 0/10 0/12 0/14 0/16 0/18 0/20 0/22

0   20m.

04. 12. 11   1m. GRID

Water flow in

praefurnium?

room 1 cald. or hot bath

room 6 natatarium

room 2 cald. or tepid.

Water flow out

room 4 frigidarium plunge apod.

room 3 tepid.

courtyard

F399

F298

F157

F204

F206

P578?

door?

F181

F391

stair

F183

steps

passage

F139

F187

room 5 latrine

F161

porch

post

cellar

F658 F659

F668

F475

F478 F479

F465

door

verandah

P318

F293

F485

F440

F131

yard

room 11 room 10 room 9 room 8

F194

eavesdrip

F553 F607

N

BUILDING 1

room 13 bakehouse?

00/0
00/2
00/4
00/6
00/8
00/10
00/12
00/14
00/16
00/18
00/20
00/22
00/24
00/26

PLAN 1

PHASE 1 (c.80AD-150AD)

—— walls
—— walls (conjectural)
—— drains & channels
—— drains & channels (conjectural)
▇ metalled surface

24. Plan of the first phase of Wortley Roman 'villa'. *David Wilson*

25. The manor house and church at Alderley – a spring-line village. *Countryside Agency: Jo Ward*

26. The space between the inner and outer defences at Little Sodbury. *Author's collection*

27. The Dyrham strip lynchet 'staircase'. *Author's collection*

28. The sad remains of Lansdown 'Sun-disc' barrow. *Author's collection*

29. The remains and reconstruction of the Lansdown 'Sun-disc'. *The Trustees of the British Museum*

30. The medieval east gate of Bath. *Author's collection*

The promontory fort on Leckhampton Hill encloses an area of about 2.8ha (7 acres), with an entrance to the east now used by the Cotswold Way. The eastern and southern sides are defined by a rampart with an outer ditch, the western and northern sides by quarried scarp edges. The results of excavations in 1925 have been clarified by further work begun in 1969. Wherever it was examined on the south side of the entrance, the rampart was found to be burnt. It was 6m (20ft) wide and up to 1.8m (6ft) high, and consisted of a stone core revetted with drystone walls tied at the base by transverse timbers. The outer wall was better preserved than the inner; it is now 1m (3ft) thick and survives to 0.5m (1.4ft) in height. A berm 1m (3ft) wide separates the rampart from 'guard chambers', formerly thought to be rectangular in plan, on either side of the entrance: despite the name they may not have had a military function and, being circular or semi-circular, they were incorporated in the in-turned ends of the rampart. Fragments of coarse Iron Age pottery retrieved during both the 1925 and 1969–71 excavation appear to indicate a very early Iron age-date construction. Romano-British pottery has been found in many places inside the fort, and five Anglo-Saxon silver pennies were found in 1924 dating from AD 853–901.

A geophysical survey was undertaken within the hill fort in August 2008. A set of linear features have been proposed to be remaining evidence of a possible land-boundary system in the central and central western sectors of the main enclosure. A set of circular features were interpreted as roundhouse-type structures and were sited in the central and south-eastern sectors of the enclosure in a discrete area, suggesting that animal farming may have been separated from human occupancy. There was also some evidence of a large earthwork aligned north-northwest to south-southeast across the central sector and possibly following the course of an earlier enclosure. Also present in the survey

27 Leckhampton Camp and Tumulus – the 'tumulus' is now though to be a late Iron Age shrine. *Edward J. Burrow, 'Ancient Entrenchments and Camps of Gloucestershire', 1924, p. 82*

SECTION 2

was evidence of ridge and furrow and the location of a Second World War radar station. The dark grass circles that are often apparent within the hill fort are fairy rings (also known as a fairy circle, elf circle, elf ring or pixie ring), and are a naturally occurring ring or arc fungi. The rings may grow to over 10m (33ft) in diameter, and they become stable over time as the fungus grows and seeks food underground.

THE CRIPPETS LONG BARROW (SO 934 173)

The pine tree-crowned Crippets Long Barrow is best seen from the gate to an underground reservoir situated next to it. The long barrow is aligned east–west and measures 57.5m (189ft) in length by 30.5m (100ft) wide by 6.1m (20 ft) high. At its east end is an excavation crater containing a flat stone 1.8m (6ft) long, indicating that it was probably the terminal chamber. Samuel Rudder, in his *New History of Gloucestershire* published in 1779, records that the barrow had been opened by workmen digging for stone.

> At a depth of 16ft (4.8m) they discovered a burial 'sepulchre' seven feet long by
> 4 feet broad and in it a perfect skeleton. The bones were fresh and firm, and the
> teeth as white as ivory. Over the head hung a helmet so corroded by rust that it
> fell to pieces on the slightest touch … This was probably the corps of some great
> man slain in war between our countrymen and the piratical Danes.

If this was the case then the Crippets Long Barrow is the most westerly pagan Saxon burial in a Neolithic long barrow.

THE DRYHILL ROMAN VILLA (SO 931 168?)

The actual site is not known with any certainty. It was excavated by W.H. Gomonde and Capt Bell in about 1849 and found to consist of twelve rooms, the largest measuring 8.2m (27ft) by 4.8m (16.5ft). There was a hypocaust, but no mosaic pavements were discovered, 'forming a great contrast to the Witcomb Villa three miles off'. There seems to have been an extensive bath building and painted walls. Coins were found ranging from the mid-third century to the late fourth century, but all finds appear to have been lost. Roman pottery, a coin and a plum bob were recently found by someone using a metal detector on a levelled area, which is said by the farmer to be the villa site, but this cannot be verified without further excavation or ploughing.

28 Crickley Hill Camp with Ermin Street below. *Edward J. Burrow, 'Ancient Entrenchments and Camps of Gloucestershire', 1924, p. 64*

29 Plan of the sequential settlements on Cleeve Hill. *Richard Savage, 'Village, Fortress, Shrine: Crickley Hill', Crickley Hill Archaeological Trust, 1988*

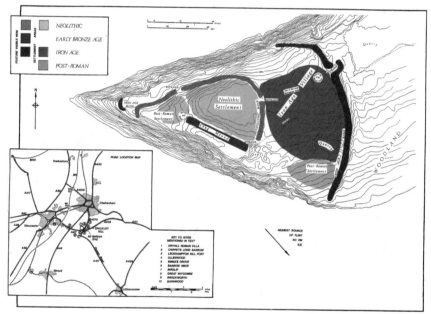

CRICKLEY HILL (CENTRED ON SO 927 160)

This triangular promontory hill fort of about 3.8ha (9.5acres) was excavated from 1969 until 1993, but unfortunately only one volume, on the defences, has been published to date. Evidence was discovered for a remarkable sequence of intermittent occupation ranging from the early Neolithic until the fifth century AD.

The first major occupation at Crickley was a causewayed enclosure identified within the centre of the hill fort interior on a flat-topped knoll, less than a hectare (2.5 acres) in area. Two lines of interrupted ditches cut off the low knoll in the centre of the promontory accompanied by low banks within the area of the later hill fort. Behind each line ran a bank built of stone taken from the ditch, through which at least two entrances had been cut. It is possible that the two circuits are contemporary, but at most they are separated by a generation. The inner ditches had been filled in and were then partially re-cut and backfilled several times, a process which implies a lengthy but intermittent use of the site. Within the interior of both phases were indications of dense occupation, with fenced roads on similar alignments, rectangular buildings and comparable gate arrangements. Later these ditches were deliberately infilled with make-up from the banks and levelled. Once the inner circuit had been filled, a more continuous ditch circuit 3m (9.8ft) wide and 1.5m (4.9ft) deep was constructed (the old ditch was still visible, but it was avoided) and a new bank was piled above it, faced with drystone walls and surmounted by a palisade. Some time after the palisade was completed, it was burnt around the whole of the circuit, and many leaf-shaped arrowheads were found in direct association. This may also be connected with the burning of all the internal structures of the enclosure. The dates from the palisade suggest that this conflict occurred probably after 3490–3450 BC.

After the c.3500 BC desertion a great linear mound in the bottom of a narrow gulley (centred at SO 926 160) was built inside the causewayed camp. It was

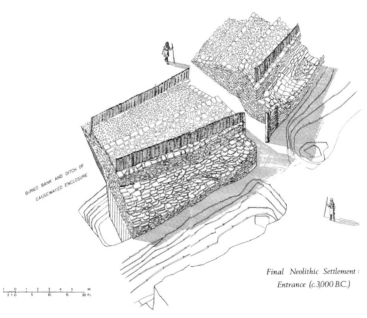

BURIED BANK AND DITCH OF CAUSEWAYED ENCLOSURE

Final Neolithic Settlement : Entrance (c.3,000 B.C.)

30 The gate of the final Neolithic settlement. *Philip Dixon and Patrcia Borne, 'Crickley Hill and Gloucestershire Prehistory', 1977*

120m (393ft) long, 4m (13ft) wide, 0.5m (1.6ft) high and, including the shallow side ditches, 12m (39ft) across, with the ends clearly defined. It consisted entirely of top soil scraped from the sides of a natural gully and seems unconnected with the local quarrying. It appears to have been modified, used and extended, but it had already assumed its present eroded shape when an Iron Age hut was built on its flank. At the end of the mound was a circle of stones with a stone slab in the centre, overlying the hearth of the possible Neolithic shrine. The slab was burnt on its upper surface and many fragments of burnt bone have been unearthed scattered around it. At the far end of the mound a short pole was erected, while the sides of the mound were marked at intervals with large slabs of stone.

No early/middle Bronze Age material has yet been found, and so after the abandonment of the Neolithic site it seems to have lain deserted until the first promontory hill fort was built around 600 BC. The new rampart and ditch enclosed some 3.6ha (9 acres), more than double that of the causewayed enclosure, and provided a substantial barrier with a rock-cut ditch 2m (6ft) deep and a drystone wall built of material taken from it at least 3m (10ft) high. The entrance was a narrow timber-lined passage shut by two gates, and the defences were presumably capped by a timber or wickerwork palisade. Behind the entrance a roadway ran between lines of large, rectangular barn-like houses and around them were granaries on four posts for the storage of crops. The evidence of wear on the roadway and the lack of need to replace the timber of the houses indicate an occupation of no more than a generation or two. The huts of this settlement, along with the gates and walls, were destroyed by fire after a short period of occupation, and again Crickley Hill was abandoned for a few years at least, while silt layers and turf formed above the ruins.

The second hill fort was commenced not later than the late sixth or early fifth century BC. Rebuilding was piecemeal as old walls were patched and a new gate inserted into the damaged entrance. Later this was replaced by a pair of solid stone bastions, a large out-turned horn-work and with gates at either end. These defences enclosed a re-planned settlement of round houses. A great round house, nearly 15m (50ft) in diameter, stood directly beyond the inner gate and around it lay an irregular ring of smaller round house with granaries and, like the first hill fort, animal pens and other agricultural structures. The new plan is much more sophisticated than the first phase, with its round houses and its pottery highly decorated and thinner, much like that being made in the Thames Valley. Despite its massive rampart the fort was attacked and captured, probably in the fifth century BC, with houses being burnt: a layer of charcoal covered the road and the walls of the bastions were reddened by fire.

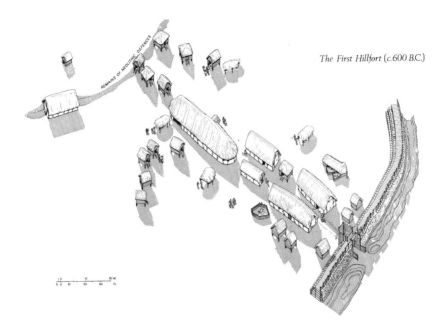

The First Hillfort (c. 600 B.C.)

31 The first hill fort at Crickley Hill. *Philip Dixon and Patrcia Borne, 'Crickley Hill and Gloucestershire Prehistory', 1977*

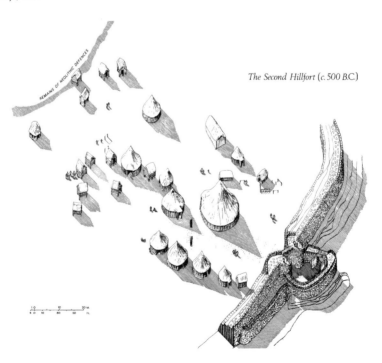

The Second Hillfort (c. 500 B.C.)

32 The second hill fort at Crickley Hill. *Philip Dixon and Patrcia Borne, 'Crickley Hill and Gloucestershire Prehistory', 1977*

Two contemporary settlements of either late Roman or sub-Roman date have been found on Crickley Hill. One was sited behind the collapsed Iron Age rampart and comprises slightly sunken huts with a narrow entrance cleared through the rampart. The other was situated 200m (656ft) to the west, on the tip of the promontory, and comprised larger buildings situated within a palisade. Both appeared to have been burnt then rebuilt, though not on the same plans. They were burnt again in the late fifth or sixth century AD. During the medieval period the northern slopes of Crickley Hill were used for grazing and a small rectangular stone-walled building may have been used as a shepherd's hut. Post-medieval features on the hill include seventeenth-century pits for lime burning, which destroyed about an acre of the prehistoric settlements, and quarrying of Pea Grit, which started in the eighteenth century and had produced steep cliffs by the early nineteenth. Quarrying was in decline by the 1930s and ceased in the 1960s.

The site is now in the ownership of the National Trust and Gloucestershire County Council as a country park. Interpretation boards, reconstructions of the ramparts and the 'footprints' of both rectangular and round huts can be seen.

THE VIEW FROM CRICKLEY HILL

The Cotswold Way at Crickley Hill is a unique place for appreciating the geography of the Roman annexation of Wales in the thirty years after AD 43. From much of the southern part of the route of the trail you can see the coastline of South Wales, with the mountainous lands behind it. It is usually seen as being the territory of the Silures, a particularly warlike and especially aggressive group of late Iron Age people. Rapid movement and mobility as the basis of Roman military might and roads would have been laid out as the troops advanced, ensuring a straitjacket of communications in areas already subdued. You can clearly see the line of Ermin Street between Cirencester and Gloucester coming down the Edge from the valley between Crickley Hill and the Air Balloon pub, marked now by the A419 road.

The Gloucester area was crucial in the invasion strategy because of its siting on the lowest crossing point of the Severn. The first military establishment in Gloucester was at Kingsholm, which lies partly beneath the rugby ground. Ermin Street was certainly surveyed with the site as its terminus, making it a very early feature in the strategic landscape. Kingsholm is considered to be a vexillation fortress, a strategic base for the assembly of operational battle groups of mixtures of legionary heavy infantry contingents and swift, mounted auxiliary troopers. It may also have been used as campaign winter quarters for troops operating in South Wales. It has often been presumed that this fortress was garrisoned by at least part of the XXth Legion, which had left Colchester in AD 49, and also groups of mounted auxiliary troopers. The fortress' defences comprised a rampart faced with turf and clay, which had a sand core and was possibly 5m (16ft) wide. In front of it was a V-shaped ditch 3.7m (12ft) wide and 1.4m (4.5ft) deep, fronted by an irregular slot containing angled stake holes, interpreted by the excavators as the remains of a thorn bush and stake emplacement. Inside the fortress evidence of timber buildings and gravelled roads and ditches has been excavated. Other evidence that the site was of military origin is the recovery of equipment, including an unfinished cheekpiece from a legionary's helmet and three cavalry pendants from horse tackle. The tombstone of Rufus Sita of the VI cohort of Thracians, mounted in armour and killing the enemy was found near Ermin Street.

From Crickley Hill you will be able to appreciate possible invasion strategies. Alongside the Severn through Lydney and Chepstow any Roman attacking force would have been hemmed in by the uplands of the Forest of Dean on one side and the river on the other, thereby making troops exceptionally vulnerable on a narrow sliver of land. Equally clear is that a safer route was to the right of the now tree-crowned May Hill and the Malverns in the valley of the Leadon, and onwards to the middle Wye Valley. Evidence of forward positions

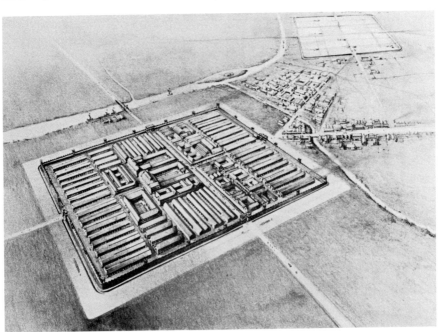

33 The fortress at Glevum with the earlier base at Kingsholm. *Philip Moss*

34 The *colonia* at Glevum. *Philip Moss*

in a strategic plan for the conquest is still lacking. Presumably the campaign forts or marching camps were very temporary structures, which may have been ploughed out or even hidden in the now wooded uplands of the Forest of Dean; there is some evidence of this emerging from LiDAR exploration of the woodlands. The Silures continued to oppose the Roman army and in the guerrilla warfare of AD 51–52 an attack left a *praefectus castrorum* (a camp prefect and third most senior member of the legion) dead; eight centurions were also killed, as well as an unspecified, but certainly significant, number of legionary soldiers. In the far distance and indicated on all of the topographs along the route you will see the Black Mountains, and at their most northern extent is the steep-sided Hay Bluff. Immediately under the Bluff was a campaign base at Clyro, a fort of the same date as Kingsholm. The distances do not look particularly great, but it took thirty years to completely pacify the Silures.

About AD 67 a new fortress was constructed on the city centre site covering *c.*17ha (43 acres) with a turf-faced rampart, timber, interval towers and a single ditch, all of which indicates that it was designed to be only a temporary installation. All the soldiers' accommodation, the barrack blocks, were of timber. The granaries have not been found yet and were probably constructed near the west gate in order to be close to the quays. A small fragment of a building identified as the headquarters, the *principia*, had a gravelled courtyard defined by foundations of stone and clay. Since the fortress was probably only garrisoned for eight or nine years as a temporary campaign base, it is unlikely that the full legion was ever in the fortress at any one time. The fortress was probably abandoned *c.*75 with the foundation of Isca Silurium at Caerleon near Newport for the II Augustan Legion.

At the close of the first century, most of the veterans who joined the legions in the 70s were probably from outside Britain. However, after twenty-five years of service most soldiers would have lost contact with their homeland and in the case of the now redundant fortress of *Glevum*, many men of the XXth Legion might have decided to return to their last posting. It was for that reason that the *colonia* at Glevum was founded on the fortress site. The development from the early *colonia* built in wood into stone-built town gives insights into the aspirations of the retired soldier population. At about AD 100, or even earlier, the ditch of the fortress was filled and its turf rampart had a stone wall inserted into its front, with limestone rubble filling the gap between them. It is likely that the gates were also rebuilt at the same time, as similar blocks of stone built in a drystone fashion were also apparent. The impression of this new design was probably meant to indicate that the fortress had turned from a temporary military establishment into a permanent town.

A *forum/basilica* on the site of the fortress *principia* became the administration centre of the *colonia*. In civilian towns the *forum* was a public space used as a small market with the *basilica* used for the meeting of the *ordo*, the council managing the town's affairs. However, the presence of a statue base in the courtyard, *c.*4m by 3m (13 ft by 10ft) and at some time carrying a bronze statue of a horse and rider, indicates a high-status formal space, which may have been less public.

There are a number of features that would be found in a Roman town close to the *forum*, but the most important would have been a temple. The position of this structure has still not been located with absolute confidence, but a row of limestone columns about 100m (109yds) long and known as the Westgate Colonnade have been found piecemeal over an extended period from the nineteenth century and has been the subject of much speculation. Since they clearly form a building of some substance, taller than the *forum/basilica* and unlikely to have been a bath building, they may well be part of a massive temple structure. Somewhere in the *colonia* would have been a baths, an imposing structure, probably as tall as the cathedral that you can see. The local peoples would have seen nothing like these massive structures before and the message that they gave was that the Roman Empire was here to stay.

A *colonia* such as Glevum had much higher legal status than a local capital such as Corinium, now Cirencester, and each might have had distinctive territories, of which the Cotswold Edge may well have been the one of the boundaries.

EMMA'S GROVE ROUND BARROWS (SO 934 159)

Three bowl barrows, known as Emma's Grove round barrows, are situated below the crest of the Cotswold Edge. Each has a depression in the centre of their mounds that is considered to be the result of unrecorded excavation.

'BIRDLIP TREASURE' ROMANO-BRITISH INHUMATION BURIALS (SO 930 151)

Near the car park at Barrow Wake, one of the most important finds of late Iron Age decorated metalwork was discovered in 1879 by quarrymen digging stone. Three skeletons, laid out with their heads to the east, were discovered buried in stone cists. The outer burials were of adult males and the central one that of a woman. The males' burials contained no grave goods, but that of the female was accompanied by the now famous Birdlip mirror, a silver-gilt brooch and two bowls made of bronze, the larger having been placed over her face. It is thought that the other may have been some sort of water clock.

The importance of the locality was demonstrated by finding another skeleton in a shallow grave about 18.2m (29yds) away lying with its head to the east, but not interred in a cist. This internment had an iron sword and the bronze rim and side plates of a bucket as grave goods. It is likely that the bucket was covering the face, demonstrating a shared burial ritual. The burials have been dated to between 50 BC and AD 47, possibly around AD 10. They may have been interred in a barrow as part of a large aristocratic burial ground which would have been largely destroyed by modern quarrying. This suggestion is supported by the supposed find of a fragment of a gold torque (a gold necklace) close by in 1947. There is no knowledge of its present whereabouts. (See plate 12.)

BIRDLIP CAMP, ALSO KNOWN AS PEAK CAMP (SO 924 150)

The promontory fort, 1ha (2.54 acres) in area, is situated in woodland occupying the projecting spur of Birdlip Hill. It comprises two curving, concentric banks that have been much reduced by quarrying, especially on the southwestern side where there is a high quarry face and the defences have been nearly obliterated by ploughing. Excavations in 1980–1 sectioned the site's outer (eastern) earthwork and trenched a small area at the promontory's western tip. The outer bank had survived to a height of only 0.3m (1ft) and no intact land surface remained beneath it. Its associated ditch proved to have

35 Cleeve, Crickley and Birdlip Camps from Great Witcombe Roman Villa. *Edward J. Burrow, 'Ancient Entrenchments and Camps of Gloucestershire', 1924, p. 5*

been re-cut four times. Each time it was displaced to the east, the new bank partly covering the previous ditch. All the ditch's phases contained sealed pottery, flintwork and bone, suggesting a Neolithic date of 2000–1000 BC. At the west end of the hill a shallow U-shaped gully, running east–west, was encountered. At the bottom lay a hearth that was overlain and sealed by a series of layers containing pottery, flints and bones. The site as a whole was reinterpreted as a Neolithic causewayed enclosure, but this is now thought to be highly speculative and based on very limited evidence.

The limestone quarrying that has damaged the causeway site produced a range of building stones, including a white shelly limestone from the Pea Grit series used in the eleventh-century work at St Peter's Abbey (now Gloucester Cathedral), a fine, hard Oolitic white freestone for internal work, especially paving, slabs and steps; a ragstone for road and a fissile stone for rough roofing slates. By the end of the 1890s it was mostly disused.

GREAT WITCOMBE ROMAN VILLA (SO 899 142)

There have been a number of excavations at Great Witcombe Villa, beginning in 1818 after its discovery by workmen removing an ash tree. Each of those excavations has left a legacy of poor preservation of the walls and foundations and unsympathetic reconstruction; therefore little of the present display represents the original positions of many aspects of the building. Phase One of the villa was a late Iron Age settlement close by, and there is the possibility that a rectangular suite of seven rooms by the stream, some with plastered walls and floors, might have been a very early villa. Elsie Clifford, in her excavations of the north-west wing, which contains the lower baths, suggested a date before the end of the first century for its construction. Since then it has been proposed that the mosaics in this phase should not be dated later than AD 200.

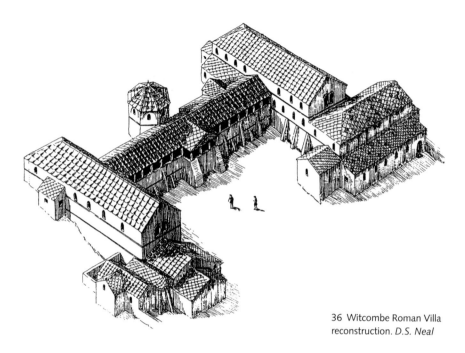

36 Witcombe Roman Villa reconstruction. *D.S. Neal*

The plan and layout of the later building was ambitious, unified and planned to impress, especially in its use of the hillside slope: it could be seen from Ermin Street as it descended the Cotswold scarp. A gallery formed the 'cross-bar' that linked the east and west wings of the 'H'-shape that framed it, giving a satisfying perspective both from and to the villa. It had a mosaic pavement flooring it and halfway along was an apsidal space later converted into an octagonal structure that may have served as a dining room. Reconstructions of the villa suggest that the gallery and both wings could have had an upper storey due to the angle of the hill side slope. However, the presence of the springs necessitated the buttressing of the gallery and the west wall of the east wing and perhaps argues against a higher structure with more weight. (See plate 13.)

The final phase, in the late third or fourth century, saw the structure become a courtyard-type villa with the addition of a southern boundary wall. It would seem that the additions and modifications to the villa structure were piecemeal, with two major episodes in the incorporation of the 'lower' baths into the south-west wing and its decoration with painted plaster and mosaics with geometrical and aquatic designs. Extensions to the south-east wings added the kitchen and stores, with possible accommodation for farm labourers. Presumably residential accommodation was on an upper floor. Additions and modifications to the house continued in the fourth century, but the basic footprint of the original design did not change. (See plate 14.)

In 2002 the Cotswold Archaeological Trust undertook a programme of field surveying, the results of which identified platforms indicating that there were further substantial ranges flanking an outer courtyard that may have incorporated a formal landscape garden and which would have further emphasised the gallery as the centre of the perspective. The villa seems to have continued into the fifth century, but in a much-dilapidated state. The subsequent hill side slumping must have been slow but dramatic, damaging the side ranges but leaving the central gallery largely intact and burying the lower parts of the site enough to protect the stratigraphy and artefacts of the south-west lower baths.

The survey work of the Cotswold Archaeological Trust in 2000 identified a number of potential structures around the house, including a possible mill. The discovery in the stream of tile wasters, indicating their manufacture, was also supported by the discovery of areas of strong magnetic response from possible kilns and hearths south and north-east of the villa, far enough away and downwind so as not to cause problems for the inhabitants. Evidence for the working of copper alloy and lead had been also been recorded previously, as well as the possibility of pewter vessels being manufactured at the villa.

Clearly, a site in such a magnificent position for flaunting wealth and status, and planned with so much care and effort to ensure the effectiveness of such spectacle, indicates an important individual of power and wealth. The rich late Iron Age burials at Barrow Wake might suggest the presence of a dynastic group, perhaps represented later by the possible mausoleum platform found during the 2000 fieldwork, which might indicate continuity from the late Iron Age into the Roman period.

The site is managed by English Heritage and is open for viewing at any reasonable time, although the mosaics are in a shed which is inaccessible.

COOPERS' HILL/HIGHBROTHERIDGE (CENTRED ON SO 890 150)

The path clips the edge of a bank and ditch which form a 'U' shape, particularly strong at SO 888 137. These are certainly of Iron Age date, as is the 'dyke' marked in Brockworth Wood. However, there have been various attempts to make a continuous feature by extending other banked and ditched features to give a 'site' covering 101ha (250 acres), claimed by some as being the largest hill fort in Britain. There are other claims for two mounds on the eastern side being the remnants of 'guardhouses' (SO 895 138), but any extension of the perimeter beyond the known stretches is quite speculative, since no reliable evidence of a rampart is visible either on the ground or in air photographs. Medieval parish boundaries and wood banks may form some of the earthworks but, as is clear, there has been much quarrying and associated hollow ways which are probably quite recent and have destroyed any evidence for a huge enclosure. Although no Iron Age pottery has been found within the perimeter even in areas which are now arable, there is still the possibility that the Iron Age earthworks form part of an unfinished enclosure which might be interpreted as a 'tribal' centre or trading hub. The existence of a possible late Iron Age structure at Great Witcombe Roman villa along with the Birdlip burials points to an area of some importance.

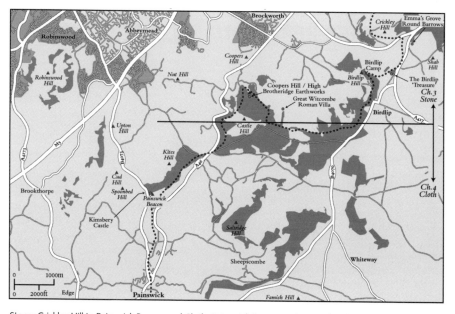

Stone: Crickley Hill to Painswick Beacon and Cloth: Painswick Beacon to Painswick and the Painswick Stream.

SECTION 3

CLOTH
PAINSWICK BEACON TO SELSLEY COMMON

THE CLOTH TRADE

During the fifteenth century, with the export of raw wool to the Continent falling off due to the wars with France, the nature of the wool trade began to change. With the decline of sheep farming in the North Cotswolds there was never an option of developing a cloth industry, as the streams that flow across the plateau into the Thames have very shallow gradients, making the use of mills very inefficient. However, around Winchcombe, Painswick, Stroud and Wotton-under-Edge deep valleys had been formed by glacial meltwaters, leaving small, 'mis-fit' streams with steep gradients, in turn producing fast-flowing streams that could provide the power for driving waterwheels. However, the major industry in the Stroud Valleys did not develop until the late sixteenth century when about 39 per cent of the men in the Bisley Hundred, which included Stroud and Painswick, were employed in the woollen industry.

Alongside the raw wool, water was the essential element in the process of making cloth. The wool was sorted and washed at the mill and drying took place in round houses. Then the dry wool was oiled and thorough mixing was achieved by a tearing operation called 'scribbling' which loosened the denser parts of the fleece. It was then distributed to the spinners, as until the advent of spinning machinery the process did not require either water or power. The spinners worked independently in their cottages on the hillsides, where the wool was carded or combed to open the fibres even more, depending on the length of the wool and the finished product for which it was used. This work was usually undertaken by children and women. The wool was then spun by

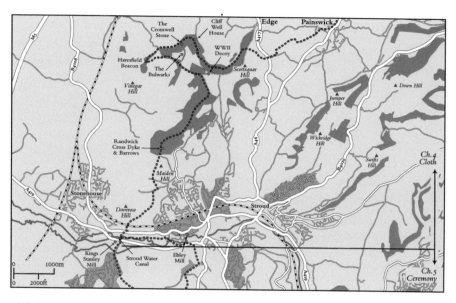

Cloth: Haresfield Beacon to Randwick Dyke and Cloth: Ebley Mill to Selsley Common to Stanley Hill and the Stroudwater Canal.

hand, 'sized' with a gluey, gelatinous solution to improve its strength and reeled into skeins. The resulting yarn was collected by the clothier or his agent for re-issue to the cottage weavers. Looms varied in width and detail according to the type of cloth to be produced. The attics of older houses were used – hence the large windows, to give more light – but after 1800–20, larger looms were often on the ground floor. With the help of his family a good weaver could produce 3.5–3.6m (10–12 ft) a day .On its return to the mill the cloth was scoured, usually with stale urine or with fuller's earth found in the central and south Cotswolds, to remove the oil and size and then partially dried on racks to remove knots, flaws and foreign bodies. It was then 'fulled' when the cloth was slowly beaten in water by wooden mallets for many hours to give a felt appearance so that the 'warp and weft' – the crossed pattern left by weaving – were no longer visible. This shrunk the cloth and made it narrower, but much thicker. After fulling the surface of the cloth was roughened by using teasels – when machinery was employed it was called 'gigging' – and a final shearing to give a smooth, uniform product. Both these processes were mechanised in the second decade of the nineteenth century. Dyeing used locally grown woad or other colours produced by madder, cochineal, indigo and crushed tropical wood fibres all imported through Bristol, often as return cargoes from cloth export. After dyeing the cloth was hung out to dry on racks in fields known as 'rack closes'.

Archaeologically, these processes leave significant traces in the landscape. On the former common land high above the valley floor are the squatter cottages of the spinners and weavers. Three storeys high, their attics formerly housed broad looms. Away from the mills, the better-class seventeenth-century houses were often built by lesser clothiers or broad weavers. However, the grander houses of the clothiers were set alongside their mills in the valley bottoms. The steep paths down the steep valley side to the mills, now lanes covered with tarmac or rights of way, were used by packhorses to transport the finished products of the spinning and weaving. The rolls of cloth from the mills reached the markets in London or Bristol by wagon, on roads high on the valley sides.

Once mechanisation had begun, the streams were vital to turn the water-wheels for fulling and gigging, and the mills were also used to store the cloth at the end of the process. The early mills were probably timber-framed, with one or two storeys and an external waterwheel at the gable end. It is possible that the remains of earlier mills are preserved by waterlogging and still lie below post-medieval structures. Often the dye houses were positioned near the mill, as in Kemp's Lane in Painswick. To ensure an ample supply of water power, mill leats – narrow open channels – conducted the water from a spring or stream to a pond. The use of leats enabled water to flow over porous sand beds without loss and ensured a supply of water to a pond that the stream would otherwise miss. Ponds were made by damming streams or excavation by hand and had sluice gates, often with rack-and-pinion mechanisms, which were installed to control the flow of water flowing onto a wheel. The sluice gates were also essential in draining the millpond for repairs. There was usually a fixed overflow weir to prevent damage in the event of thunderstorms or the mill being washed away when the dam burst. At the close of the eighteenth century, iron began to replace wood in the making of parts of the water mills, which as a result became larger and more powerful. Ponds were further altered to supply more water. It was not unusual for several wheels to be running side by side or for the wheel to be supplemented by Boulton and Watt steam engines which could be coupled to the waterwheel shafting.

Practically every cloth mill along the west escarpment of the Cotswolds was rebuilt in the twenty years after 1800. The old one- or two-storeyed mills were replaced by much larger structures which had spinning machines and power looms for weaving. The industry moved downstream to the Stroud area and mills with four or five floors developed. With better access to transport after the opening of the Stroudwater Canal, built between 1775 and 1779, the mills of the Frome valley towards Painswick were made redundant for clothmaking. Many of these mills used their water power for corn or the manufacture of umbrella sticks, making pins or walking sticks, often changing between products in response to market forces. Now only the silted-up millponds and owners' houses survive as evidence of a once flourishing industry.

KIMSBURY CASTLE (SO 869 122)

The fort on Painswick Beacon has been known as Kimsbury and Kingsbarrow Castle and is one of the smaller multivallate hill forts in Gloucestershire. There has been no archaeological excavation so there is no evidence of what form the occupation took or how long it lasted, but it is typical of forts in southern Britain which date to *c*.440–100 BC. The interior of the fort is about 3ha (7 acres) and resembles an irregular parallelogram, measuring a maximum 370m (404yds) south-west to north-east and 250m (273yds) across its broad, western end. Three banks and ditches defend the western, southern and eastern sides. There appears to have been at least one bank and ditch on the north side, although this and the east sides have been destroyed by quarrying. The defences are stronger to the west, where the ramparts measure *c*.60m (196ft) across and rise *c*.14m (46ft) from the base of the outer bank to the crest of the inner bank. The situation is similar on the southern side and in both areas the steep natural slope was modified. To the east the defences are comparatively slight – the exterior ground level is only a few metres below the interior level of the hill fort – with the varying scales of defence determined by the natural ground surface. 'Entrances' to the south-west, north-west and east may possibly be associated with medieval or post-medieval haul roads serving quarries within the interior. The in-turned south-east entrance which is enclosed between two exterior banks appears to be contemporary with the

37 Kimsbury Camp on Painswick Beacon. *Edward J. Burrow, 'Ancient Entrenchments and Camps of Gloucestershire', 1924, p. 99*

construction of the hill fort, but the area has been mutilated by quarrying and the original plan cannot be ascertained. A rusty sword and some spearheads were found here in about 1749, as have Roman coins at various times. About 1921 Iron Age pottery, a bronze harp-shaped fibula brooch (dating from aound 200 BC) and some third-century AD red-and-black pottery were discovered near the fort. The Roman artefacts may just be stray losses from casual visits or gathering stone for the walls of local villas. (See plate 15.)

During the Second World War an observation post was set up on the golf course within the hill fort and the remains can be seen near the 6th hole. It consisted of reinforced, corrugated steel sheets bolted together to make a Nissen hut and was covered with earth and stones to hide it from enemy aircraft. Only one end was visible and this was bricked up except for the door. Inside was an earth floor with a table and chairs, and at the back a pair of bunks for the off-duty guard. Light was provided by a paraffin lamp. A field telephone communicated with the command centre in the Town Hall. A squad consisted of four men on duty from 9pm to 6am with a rifle and five live rounds of ammunition. Apparently, it was possible to see the glow of the fires burning in Coventry and Bristol after air raids.

THE VIEW FROM PAINSWICK BEACON (SO 869 120)

In the distance you can see May Hill, with its tree clump first planted in the mid-eighteenth century and a circle of 1.6ha (4 acres) once reserved 'for the recreation of the inhabitants of Longhope and its neighbourhood'. Since then trees have been added to the clump to mark the Golden Jubilee of Queen Victoria in 1887 and that of Queen Elizabeth II of 1977. The prominence and visibility of 'natural' places seems to have been important during the late Iron Age, if not well before, as that might be why *you* are also walking this route. Red sandstone from the immediate area of May Hill was used for querns to grind corn to make flour, and are found much more frequently in this area than where May Hill was not visible. The acquisition of these querns may have a mystical importance rather than just a purely functional or economic one, and it is noteworthy that a fragment of a May Hill quern was found in a pit at the Iron Age–Roman temple at Uley.

As a result of rising sea levels in south-west Britain since glacial times salt marshes have developed, consisting of sediment brought by the tides along the Severn. The resulting wetland landscapes were highly suitable for the grazing of livestock on the marshes and fishing and it is also likely that there was pro-duction of salt through boiling sea water. In the late Iron Age and early Roman period these areas might have remained wetland and been managed for wild-fowling or seasonal use for cattle grazing. However, in the area of Elmore from the late Iron Age through to medieval and early modern periods, reclamations have been undertaken through drainage of land by cutting ditches as well as controlling, widening or diverting existing natural streams. Fieldwork has also identified a considerable body of evidence to indicate the building of massive sea defences like the late Roman period 'Great Wall', which is still detectable in the landscape in Elmore parish. Research has also demonstrated that at least half of the 29sq/km (11.2sq miles) of reclaimed wetlands in the upper estuary were of this late Roman date. Settlement on this new alluvial farmland has been located through field walking and the discovery of large scatterings of building materials indicating single substantial farmsteads, probably of extended families, rather than villages. No site has produced evidence of mosaics or hypocausts and the lack of tile would suggest that roofs were thatched using reeds from the river.

You may think that the 'outliers' of the Cotswold Ooltic escarpment at Robinswood and Churchdown Hill look perfect for hill forts, with their position controlling the landscape. However, there is no evidence of an Iron Age site on the former, and very debatable traces on the latter.

PAINSWICK (CENTRED ON SO 865 950)

The name *Wic* generally means 'settlement', while the prefix *Pain* is believed to have been derived from the name of the lord of the manor in the twelfth century, Pain FitzJohn. The medieval settlement at Painswick developed along the course of the main route that linked Gloucester with Bisley and Cirencester, and which would have entered the town along the modern line of Gloucester Street, followed Bisley Street and left Painswick to Bisley via Tibbiwell Street or Vicarage Street. The church was built to the south-west of the main through route during the eleventh century, or possibly earlier. A small castle is believed to have been built at Painswick during the twelfth century, possibly during the period when Pain FitzJohn held the manor, though there are neither visible remains of the castle nor any indication of the nature of its fortifications. The manor house is thought also to have stood to the south of the church, in the area of the castle, and was in use as a residence until the fifteenth century. Both structures would have commanded the southern approach into the town.

The medieval market was held in the area that now lies in the junction of Bisley Street and St Mary's Street. It is possible that the market may originally have extended as far south-west as the churchyard, forming a roughly

38 Painswick church – the churchyard is full of exquisite memorials. *Countryside Agency: Nick Turner*

rectangular area through which all traffic between Gloucester and Cirencester would have been forced to pass. The area has since been built up by infilling which is likely to have begun during the peak of the market's prosperity. Vicarage Street is also thought to have been built up during the earlier medieval period, as it was one of the ways in which travellers could pass through the town. In 1429, New Street was laid out to the north-west of the church-yard, providing a more direct route between Gloucester and Stroud,

The new road was created in response to the increasing importance of Stroud in the cloth industry, but it also served to alter the focus of the settlement at Painswick westwards, away from the marketplace towards the north-western corner of the churchyard. The north side of New Street has a range of buildings of different dates. Only the Post Office has exposed timber-framing to demonstrate its early origins, though many houses are timber-framed inside. The important route to Stroud through the town, and the position across from the parish church, made this side of New Street prestigious and many of the medieval structures were demolished or modified with new facades, particularly in the nineteenth century.

St Mary's Church, containing topiary yews set out c.1792, should be more famous for its collection of some 230 tombs, mostly dating from the eighteenth century. A wide variety of designs, progressing from the upright headstone to the massive horizontal ledger, the chest, the pedestal and the 'tea caddy', are to be found in the churchyard. The inscribed names reflect the social history of Painswick, and the vigorous commercial life of the town is represented by the mill owners, salters, a timber merchant, an army captain, a druggist, an apothecary, a nurseryman, bakers, tallow chandlers, farmers, butchers, cordwainers and maltsters, though only one servant is represented.

39 Painswick Post Office – one of the few buildings retaining its medieval timber frontage. *Countryside Agency: Nick Turner*

It was during the seventeenth and eighteenth centuries that Painswick prospered through the cloth trade, and this is reflected in the nature of the buildings constructed and the general expansion of the settlement at this time. Most of the cloth mills lay along the course of the Painswick Brook to the east of the town, and their success, combined with the crossing point over the Painswick Stream at the eastern end of Tibbiwell Lane, played an important role in encouraging the development of the eastern side of the town. Tibbiwell Lane and Vicarage Street thus began to be developed, mainly by the weaving community, who found it convenient to be close to the mills.

Sixteen mills have been recorded adjoining the parish on the Painswick Stream (formerly 'Wycke Stream'), which rises in Cranham Woods and eventually joins the River Frome. Its tributaries, the Sheepscombe Brook, the Washwell Brook and the Pitchcombe Brook, have documentary evidence for thirty-one mills – twenty-seven in the cloth trade. The footpath along the Painswick Stream from the bottom of Vicarage Lane gives an insight into the changes in products through time depending on economic conditions.

Brookhouse Mill stands by Greenhouse Lane. The buildings date from the seventeenth century, but they were substantially rebuilt and enlarged during the late eighteenth and nineteenth centuries. In the eighteenth century it worked as a cloth mill with a dye-house. Although steam power was introduced by 1822, the growing importance of Stroud saw the mill become an umbrella-stick factory. By 1853, Brookhouse Mill worked as a corn mill, but by 1879 it had been converted for use as a hairpin factory. The mill remained a pin mill, which employed *c.*300 people in 1904. A waterwheel, although supplemented by a gas engine, remained in use to provide power until 1962 and was broken up two years later, not because of wear and tear, but due to sediment and land reclamation reducing the size of the pond.

Cap Mill is 182m (200yds) downstream of Brookhouse Mill. A fulling mill with two stocks, a gig, and a dye house existed in 1622. In 1853 it was converted for use as a pin mill, but by 1867 it was used as a sawmill. The mill house, a tall, gabled house, is an excellent example of a rich clothier's house.

Painswick Mill stands downstream of Cap Mill on Knap Lane. The mill was apparently worked in the 1630s and operated as a cloth mill in 1820. By 1863 it had been converted for use as a pin mill. The mill buildings had been demolished by 1972, but the mill-owner's house, a three-storey gabled structure built in 1634 with nineteenth-century additions, survived near the site.

Skinner's Mill above Stepping Stone Lane was possibly a mill working in the sixteenth and seventeenth centuries. By 1885, steam power had been introduced to the mill, which continued in use for milling cattle feed until the 1920s. The house and mill, which form a single building, are mostly of the later seventeenth and nineteenth centuries, but they incorporate medieval, probably late fourteenth-century, elements.

In Kemp Lane, leading back into the town, is a cylindrical drying house.

CLIFF WELL HOUSE, HARESFIELD (SO 832 096)

This stone-built well house is dated 1870 and has a steep, pitched, tiled roof and an archway enclosed by a locked iron gate. There is a trapdoor over the well hand-winding gear still inside.

40 Cliff Well. *Author's collection*

There is an inscription on the back wall that reads:

> Deo Gratias
> Whoer the Bucketful upwindeth,
> Let him bless God, who Water findeth;
> Yet water here but small availeth,
> Go seek that which never faileth
> John C4 V14

On the back of the entrance walls, looking out from the inside, on the left side is a panel with a sliver of a moon and stars around it and the inscription:

CAVE ADEST NOX
('Beware of being consumed by the night').

On the right side is a sun with face and rays and the inscription:

INSTAT DIES TRANSIT NOX
('Every moment of the day passes into night').

Looking at the external walls of the entrance from the front are two cartouches –on the right: A C N (?); on the left: J D. Both are, presumably, the initials of the builders or whoever commissioned the structure. There is another cartouche high up on the side of the structure, which is the Star of David.

SECTION 3

THE CROMWELL STONE (SO 829 096)

A boundary marker on the north side of the path below, known as the 'Cromwell' stone, is inscribed on both sides and dated 1870s. It supposedly marks the point from which Oliver Cromwell watched the lifting of the siege of Gloucester in the First English Civil War. It took place between 3 August and 5 September 1643, with the army of King Charles I besieging the Parliamentarian garrison of Gloucester. The siege was lifted when a Parliamentarian relief column under the Earl of Essex arrived to aid their comrades. The Royalist forces withdrew, having suffered heavy losses.

The stone's inscription reads:

SIEGE OF
GLOUCESTER
5th SEPTEMBER
1643

THE VIEW FROM HARESFIELD BEACON (SO 822 090)

Haresfield triangulation pillar is a superb position to appreciate the importance of the River Severn in the landscape, and the large meander at Arlingham is a useful reference point to explore the estuary and lower reaches of the river. The River Severn, the Roman *Sabrina*, must have been of special mystical significance due to its surge wave or 'bore'. The shape of the Severn Estuary is such that the water is funnelled into an increasingly narrow channel as the tide rises, thus forming the large wave. At spring tides the wave attains a height of up to 7.5m (25ft) and a speed of 24–27km/h (13–15 knots). If you have seen the Severn Bore, although expected and explained, you will have felt its raw, frightening power as it moves upstream, bludgeoning the reeds at the top of the bank. Even more so is the roaring sound, which has been heard advancing at a range of 22km (14 miles). The effect on people in the prehistoric past must have been dramatic, and there must have been a deity of the bore and ritual sites to placate it. Perhaps one of these is the late Iron Age and Roman temple at Lydney.

The Severn has been important throughout history as the through route to the Midlands. In the Iron Age, pottery came up from the Somerset Levels, and coins from Armorica, Northern Brittany and from Massalia on the southeastern coast of modern day France, have been found in settlements along the river. The Severn Valley Ware pottery industry, using the alluvial clays of the valley floor, was active through the late Iron Age and most of the Roman period from Thornbury to Worcester. Pottery is heavy and fragile, as well as being shaped in curves that do not fit together easily, resulting in many breakages; however, transport by water is much easier for bulk quantities and results in fewer breakages. In the second and third centuries, Severn Valley Ware was used on the west end of the Antonine Wall from the River Clyde to the Firth of Forth in Scotland, the pottery being transported by sea.

Today the River Severn has an extreme tidal range, the second highest rise and fall in the world, and even from the Cotswold Way the great bends of the Arlingham meander can be seen to have extensive and hazardous sand banks, which, along with rocks just below the surface, cause havoc for vessels. A way of avoiding the turbulent tides of the River Severn was the digging of the Sharpness to Gloucester Canal, which you can identify by the towers at each end – to the left the 1930s grain silo at Sharpness and to the right Gloucester Cathedral. It was planned as the deepest and widest canal in the country, and opened on 26 April 1827. The ship canal was intended to provide a safe route for local traffic at all states of the tide, as well as allowing sea-going ships to reach Gloucester where cargoes could be transferred directly to inland canal boats, thus enabling the city to challenge Bristol as a primary port.

41 The patterns of ridge and furrow seen from the air around Haresfield Beacon. *Martin Ecclestone, 'The Haresfield Pottery: an investigation', Glevensis Review, 33:2000, p. 51*

Above the Arlingham Bends at Framilode on the south bank the Stroudwater Canal was built as a branch canal from the nearest navigable waterway, the River Severn. Begun in 1774–75, it was one of the earliest canals in Britain and was built to carry bulk loads of coal coming from the pits of Shropshire and Staffordshire to the woollen mills of the Stroud valleys. The Stroudwater Canal and the ship canal from Sharpness to Gloucester crossed each other at Junction locks near Whitminster. (See plate 16.)

RING HILL FORT (SO 822 090)

This site demonstrates the problems of identifying archaeological earthworks, particularly when they are unexcavated and in areas of quarrying. The enclosure on Ring Hill has been described as being a univallate hill fort, without a ditch, enclosing nearly 4ha (10 acres) at the end of a spur. The north and south sides are defined by a bank up to 9m (30ft) wide and 1.2m (4ft high) set along the scarp edges. On the east side the bank rises to follow the crest of a natural ridge above a gully. The west end, at the tip of the spur, and formerly the site of a beacon, is disturbed. The enclosure has five entrances approached from below by hollow ways and terrace ways, but a break in the bank at the southeast angle, affording access from the plateau, appears to be modern. It has been argued that the 'Bulwarks' to the east were known as 'Eastbury', suggesting that Ring Hill may have been 'Westbury', in which case the Bulwarks would have formed a contemporary annexe to the fort, trebling the area enclosed.

Nonetheless, ramparts anywhere without a single trace of a ditch are suspicious; especially when too insubstantial for defence. Ring Hill has obviously been subjected to extensive surface quarrying in the past, although most of it has now been brought back to arable or rough pasture. In the circumstances there is no detail remaining on the hill that cannot be explained away in the light of these activities; even the supposed entrances can be shown to coincide with tracks coming onto the hill from medieval and later occupation in the valleys below.

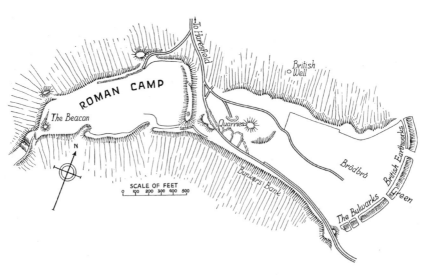

42 Haresfield Beacon showing the 'Roman Camp', which was most probably of the same date as the middle Iron Age Bulwarks. The Roman presence was more likely to have been civilian or religious, not military. *Edward J. Burrow, 'Ancient Entrenchments and Camps of Gloucestershire', 1924, p. 75*

Casual finds tell a different story and the evidence points strongly to the occupation of Ring Hill during the Roman period. A collection composed of twelve bags of unstratified pottery has been collected randomly where there has been animal disturbance of the soil, and is largely composed of third- and fourth-century material. A number of pieces of ceramic building materials are also present in the collection, which includes the various forms of Roman roofing tiles. A coin hoard is recorded as found in 1837 at a location near the south gate of the camp earthworks, mostly belonging to the period AD 306 to 343, along with several Roman horseshoes, the antlers of a red deer and bone needles. Recent finds include a trumpet fibula brooch, a penannular brooch, an incomplete buckle and coins of Tetricus I (253–260), Gallienus (271–274) and Constantine I (306–337).

In 2010, a geophysical survey of the central part of the Ring Hill Camp was undertaken. It identified a possible platform of high resistance – whether this was as a building platform or a high area of the local bedrock of the area is uncertain – and the presence of a number of possible wall lines crossing the interior of the hill fort. The site of a probable Roman building occurs at SO 823 090, inside the earthworks on Ring Hill, with a scatter of pottery, tile fragments and limestone slabs suggesting an occupation near the east entrance in the south side of the 'fort'. The site might seem perfect for an Iron Age hill fort and rather windswept for Roman settlement. However, considering the nature of the finds, which could easily be votive offerings, there might well be a Roman temple on the promontory overlooking the River Severn.

Haresfield Tumulus (SO 820 088)

This is another feature of considerable controversy. It is about 18m (60ft) in diameter and 2m (6.5ft) high and was recorded as a round barrow by Witts: 'Haresfield Beacon: within the entrenchments of Haresfield Camp'. However, it has also been considered to be a feature of the Iron Age camp or may represent a natural ground anomaly, being located below the level of the interior of Ring Hill, on geologically unstable ground causing landslipping and foundered strata.

BUNKERS BANK ANTI-TANK CYLINDERS (SO 831 087)

Alongside many roads in the area are concrete blocks that have been formed by pouring cement and aggregate into corrugated roofing formed into a cylinder shape. The Bunkers Bank bollards are the remains of anti-tank defences that ran around Bristol, known as Stop-Line Green and designed to keep the port of Bristol open for evacuation or re-supplying and reinforcing the city if it was attacked.

43 Second World War anti-tank cylinders at Bunker's Bank. *Author's collection*

THE BULWARKS (CENTRED ON SO829 091)

The Bulwarks appears to be a hill fort, consisting of a single bank with an outer ditch crossing the neck of the spur 576m (630yds) east of Ring Hill. There are four gaps in the bank which have related causeways across the ditch, but it is unlikely that any of them are original. The site has not been excavated, but a few fragments of indeterminate hand-made pottery were found in the field to the west of the bank. The Bulwarks has been considered to be an encampment which may have possibly formed a contemporary annexe to the hill fort on Ring Hill.

COLD WAR OBSERVATION BUNKER (SO 829 087)

During the Second World War the Royal Observer Corps was important in identifying enemy air strikes from above ground positions, but by 1955 the body went into protected accommodation and undertook the monitoring of radioactive fallout in the event of a nuclear strike on the United Kingdom, the resultant warnings being issued to the military and civilian population alike. The Stroud post on Haresfield Hill, 91.5m (100yds) north-west of the National Trust car park was in use from April 1963 and October 1968. It was re-opened two years later in November 1970 when the Barnwood post was closed and it was in use until September 1991 when the bulk of the Royal Observer Corps, approximately 9,600 members, was stood down. It was then demolished, leaving no trace of anything today; the location is marked as 'reservoir' on some maps. Complete examples can be seen at Broadway Tower (SP 114 361) and near Horton (ST 766 838).

STANDISH SECOND WORLD WAR BOMBING DECOY (SO 835 085)

A shelter for the control of a bombing decoy still exists alongside the road junction a few hundred metres east of the Haresfield Beacon car park. It survives as an overgrown earthen mound with a blast wall protecting an entrance tunnel and steps, now blocked off. The bunker, built in January 1941, was part of a 'Permanent Starfish' (the name came from the original code, SF, for Special Fire) site, which was designed to replicate the railway marshalling yards of Gloucester and thereby deflect enemy bombing. They were operated by lighting a series of controlled fires, ignited electronically from such a remote shelter or control building during an air raid, in this case to simulate locomotive glows. During 1942 a 'QL' decoy was incorporated into the site using lights travelling on a rig across the field which could simulate the shunting activities of the engines. The Standish example has circular holes in the sides facing the field, which may have been for the cables associated with these techniques (often known as 'hares and hounds'). The site was in use until 1943. (See plates 17 and 18.)

RANDWICK DYKE (SO 827 070)

The section of the route above the Frome Valley seems to have especial ritual significance, with three elements: a cross dyke and behind it two *tumuli* and a long barrow. The relationship between the four is shown on an interpretation board alongside the track. On the opposite spur above Selsley Common is a similar arrangement of a cross dyke, round and long barrows.

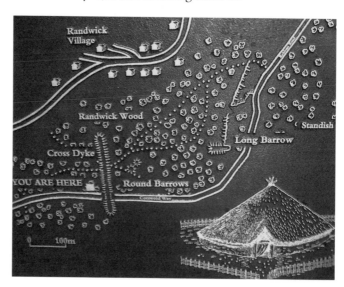

44 The Randwick
Monuments
interpretation board.
Author's collection

Witts named it 'Randwick Camp'; however, it is best seen as a 'cross dyke' consisting of a single bank and ditch 200m (600 ft) long, with no original gap. It runs across the neck of the hill, with each end resting on the escarpment. The bank averages 3.7m (12ft) wide by 0.7m (2.5ft) high; the ditch uphill on the east averages 0.6m (2.3ft) deep, the bank 0.7m (2.5ft) high. Construction of cross dykes, as revealed by excavation and by analogy with associated monuments, appears to span a millennium from the middle Bronze Age, though they may have been reused later. Current interpretation suggests they were used as territorial limits and/or as internal boundaries and land allotment within communities.

TUMULI (CENTRED ON SO 826 069)

Two ditched round barrows are within the cross dyke. One is 10m (33ft) in diameter by 0.5m (1.5ft) high, and the other 11m (36ft) in diameter by 0.9m (3ft) high. Neither has been excavated.

RANDWICK LONG BARROW (SO 824 069)

Whereas it is often difficult to find the round barrows because of the lack of light, there are no trees on this long barrow and at every season of the year it stands out like a bright green stranded whale amid the dark undergrowth around it. The long barrow is orientated east-north-east to west-south-west and is highest, 4m (13ft), at its east end. Unfortunately, the lack of obstacles has caused it to be attractive to mountain bikers, who are damaging the monument. Before excavation in 1883 by Witts and Witchell its west end had been quarried away, leaving it 34.5m (113 ft) in length. Between the horns of the barrow at its east end was a single burial chamber which contained the fragmented remains of at

least seven skeletons, with some pottery. Above these, two pieces of Roman pottery – with the mark of the potter and a well-formed

45 Randwick Long Barrow, with mountain-bike erosion tracks. *Author's collection*

rim – and a Roman horseshoe were discovered in what 'undoubtedly was the principal chamber of this Long Barrow'. The barrow had been surrounded by a drystone wall and other internal walls, possibly used to stabilise the mound, were unearthed within it. Several crouched long-headed skeletons, in a fragmented state, were uncovered against the south revetment wall *c.*2.4m (8ft) from the quarry face at the west end. Witts reported the 'Dolicho-cephalic' character of the skulls and the sitting positions in which they were placed:

> It was the custom to bury slaves and retainers as near as possible to those of their chiefs, and if they were unable to get leave to place them in the Barrow, they placed them as near as possible to the external wall, just as we found them.

Witts sought to explain the presence of Roman objects:

> That the Romans excavated in this chamber I have no doubt whatever; and we have probably to thank some far-seeing Roman officer for the fact that they left their cards in the shape of a horse shoe and some pottery, to inform future archaeologists that they had already explored this portion of the Barrow. I further maintain that these Roman Archaeologists were guilty of removing the skulls and femurs. And what would be more natural? They no doubt presented them as great curiosities (just as we do now) to the museums of Glevum (present-day Gloucester) and Corinium (present-day Cirencester)!

As a 'scientist', Witts' archaeological reports are always highly serious and objective and we can only accept that his final remark is not 'tongue-in-cheek'!

Above Randwick Woods, the view shows a major landscape transformation and, accompanying it, a significant change in the archaeology. The sheer bulk of Stanley Mill (clearly designed to be viewed from the north) and Ebley Mills indicate the growth of scientific and engineering power, causing a change in lifestyles, power and hierarchy, set out in the landscape.

STANLEY MILL (SO 812 043)

Two mills were recorded in Domesday Book of 1086, and they were the most valuable of those mentioned in the county. One or both probably occupied the site of Stanley Mill on the Frome, which was perhaps the ruinous mill recorded on the manor in 1322. The site remained in use as a corn mill until the building of the present structure. In 1813 the old mill had been dismantled and the foundations of the new one begun, powered by five waterwheels (placed

46 King's Stanley Mill: beauty and practicality. *Photograph copyright of Amanda B. Slater*

inside the mill in order to protect them from the deliberate damage that sometimes occurred during water disputes). A steam engine had been installed by 1827. In the summer of 1834 the supply of water to the wheels was so irregular that the mill could not operate efficiently, and by 1839 the steam engine had been increased to 50 horse power. In 1839 there were ninety handlooms at work in the mill, employing 132 workers, about half of them women and children. Water power was used until the 1930s to drive a turbine to provide electricity.

The building combines practical utility with beauty. Fire was a constant hazard in woollen mills as a result of large amounts of grease and oil gradually soaking into the wooden floors and a combination of candles, gas and paraffin jets used for lighting. Stanley Mill's five-storeyed L-block has a very early fireproof construction. Heavy iron doors with self-closing weights are fitted to staircase doorways. The design was so successful that the mill survived a major fire in 1884. The influence of the Stroudwater Canal is seen in the transport of bricks from the London Brick Company, the ironwork from Dudley in the Midlands and slate for the roof from North Wales. The fireproofed structure of Stanley Mill was used to advantage in the Second World War when it became a munitions store. A central arcade of double rows of cast-iron Doric columns with a round-arched tracery provided a substantial backbone for the building, supporting brick vaults and stone floors, and the

47 King's Stanley Mill: fire-proof design. *Photograph copyright of Amanda B. Slater*

spandrels of the tracery above the arcade were of a correct size to take power drive shafts. These Greek-derived columns demonstrate the owner's pretensions and aspirations through the choice of classical architecture for an industrial building. (See plate 20.)

The mill was closed in 1989 and in 2010 was on an English Heritage register as 'at risk', which motivated Stroud District Council to grant planning permission for 135 houses and flats.

SELSLEY COMMON ALTERNATIVE ROUTE

Archaeologically, it is more rewarding to take the alternative route along the Stroudwater Canal and onto Selsley Common. Although the Cotswold Way does not go through King's Stanley (centred SO 810 035), it is worth noting that the settlement has a rare continuity of importance from the prehistoric period to the present day. Several hundred prehistoric flints were recovered during the excavations in the grounds of Leonard Stanley House in the late 1980s and are thought to represent activity through the Mesolithic, Neolithic and Bronze Age periods. During excavations in the churchyard at King's Stanley Iron Age pottery, post holes and a gravel surface were recovered, as well as a circular pit containing a tightly flexed female skeleton and pottery of late Iron Age/early Roman date. A Roman structure lies to the north of, and probably beneath, the church and churchyard, but there is no evidence for mosaic pavements or painted wall plaster, indicating that the structure was relatively modest. The remains may be been a temple or shrine, since six uninscribed altars were found at King's Stanley in 1781 when a cellar was dug. Three carry representations of Mars as god of agriculture, the fourth depicts a genius, a guiding spirit or 'guardian angel' and the fifth portrays an armed deity, probably British.

THE STROUDWATER CANAL (SO 818 048)

The waterway between the River Severn and the woollen mills of Stroud was built between 1775 and 1779 as the Stroudwater Canal. It was the third in a series of attempts, with the earlier ones using the River Frome; one of these tried to resolve the conflict of interest with the millers over water rights by using containers which were craned over the mill weirs. This is probably the first documented transport system which used containerisation – unfortunately early eighteenth-century technology was not up to the job and it failed.

48 The Stroudwater Canal under renovation. *Photograph copyright of Tom Vivian*

49 A new lock gate's paddle gear. *Photograph copyright of Tom Vivian*

50 The manufacturing history of a lock gate. *Photograph copyright of Tom Vivian*

It was planned as a broad canal designed to take a vessel that could carry 101mt (100 tons). The canal successfully captured a considerable amount of local trade, mainly supplying coal to the many mills in the Stroud Valley. The Abandonment Act was passed in 1954 and the canal suffered a great deal of damage in the twenty years that followed. The Stroudwater Canal Society was formed in 1972 and spearheaded a campaign for its restoration. The organisation developed into the Cotswold Canal Partnership, with Stroud District Council taking on the role of lead partner. (See plate 19.)

The Cotswold Way is routed from the Ryeford Double Locks to Oil Mill along the towpath, which was re-opened, levelled and surfaced alongside the completely excavated canal channel in May 2008. The Ryeford lock chambers (So 818 046) were repaired in December 2010, being completed in November 2011 when new lock gates were in place.

The Oil Mill (SO 826 045) on the River Frome was built in 1721 to produce rape and linseed oil, but was adapted to a fulling mill between 1727 and 1751, continuing in cloth production for more than 100 years. The present brick building dates partly from 1791 and partly from the nineteenth century. In 1856 it ceased to be a cloth mill and became a corn mill. It is now the home of Snow Business International Ltd, which creates artificial snow for the film industry.

EBLEY MILL (SO 826 045)

The Ebley and Stanley Mills were at times owned by the same person and even shared cloth-making processes and histories, which are reflected in the common elements in their architecture. That this was also a favourable site is indicated by the presence of a mill here as early as 1393. The river provided the full power of the combined Stroud and Nailsworth streams and in the fifteenth and sixteenth centuries the mill was used for corn grinding, with the fulling of cloth also undertaken on the site, a common arrangement at the time. A survey of 1744 recorded the freestone mansion house, an outhouse used as a dyehouse and the mill with four fulling stocks and a teasel-raising gig. The decline of the mill began with the building of the canal, which cut across the river, forcing the moving of the weir and the creation of a new waste channel. Part of the millpond was also filled in and now there is no trace of the mill, or the river loop on which it was built. It was only after the profitable years of the French wars, when the mill was involved in manufacturing uniforms for the army, that a great new building was erected. The Long Building, also known as the New Mill, was built between about 1818 and 1820, to the south of the Old Mill. It was one of the new generation of wide-bodied mills which

51 Ebley Mill now Stroud District Council Offices. *Author's collection*

continued the tradition of being rectangular, but was almost twice as wide as mills of the previous century.

Sometime before 1825, 2.8ha (7 acres) on the south side of the river were flooded and a weir was built across the waste channel. The weir created a 1.8m (6ft) fall of water which was run under the mill to drive five watermills, each with a diameter of 4.8m (16ft). These were housed on the ground floor along with the fulling stocks and the gig mills. Effectively, the mill had become a bridge over a complex water system. The Old Mill was used for scouring the raw wool and seventy-one handlooms were housed in a neighbouring building. Probably the Long Building, with its five storeys, housed processes like carding and spinning that could benefit from waterpower. In *c.*1840 the Greenaway Building to the west was constructed, five floors tall and ten bays long. Today the buildings between these major elements might represent surviving parts of the Old Mill of 1800.

The danger of fire was realised when in 1852 a hole the height of the structure and 6m (20ft) wide was blown in the front wall of the Long Building, and in 1859 a part of the block was destroyed by a massive fire which caused £20,000 worth of damage. This resulted in a new building, Bodley's Block (named after the designer), which backed on to the Long. Its design reflects the need for better light and the higher ceilings demanded by the new machinery, and because it housed a steam engine, the chimney was in a safe position separate from the main structure. An impressive fire-proof staircase turret, reminiscent of a French chateau, was built in the angle between the Bodley and the Long Buildings, servicing both and being the only access point between the two. In 1938 Ebley Mill switched to electric power and the last waterwheel and steam engine were soon scrapped, though the back brook continued to run along the west of the mill. The mill was purchased by Stroud District Council in 1986 for conversion into new, centralised offices and the course of the brook is under the present entrance road. The new structure treats the mill buildings sympathetically and the new additions are sensitively designed to reflect the old, but using new materials. The renovated mill building was fully opened in 1990.

Both Stanley and Ebley Mills survived by adapting to changing needs, producing high-quality wool products as well as fibres such as nylons, polyesters and polyamides.

STROUD (SO 850 053)

There is little surviving evidence of the medieval community. The church dedicated to St Lawrence was largely rebuilt in 1866–8. The earliest settlement may have been between The Cross at the end of High Street and the present junction of High Street and Kings Street. There was no recorded market until 1570, and the Market House, now the Town Hall, was erected in 1590. Any medieval market serving the surrounding villages may have been in The Shambles between High Street and the churchyard, but also possibly along High Street, which is wide enough for lines of stalls. The town expanded greatly in the nineteenth and twentieth centuries, absorbing the surrounding medieval villages, and this rapid growth has been based almost completely on the importance of the textile industry.

VIEW FROM SELSLEY COMMON (SO 827 030)

You may find that this panorama has a quality of 'looking in' rather than 'looking out'. Glacial meltwaters took advantage of the numerous weak spots provided by faulting of the limestone to cut a course through the Cotswold escarpment, resulting in the River Frome. The erosive action of the Frome caused its tributaries, which also exploited the faulting system, to cut deep valleys and created deeply embayed valleys with fast-flowing streams. However, the use of the route by the canal, road and railway systems developed the industry of the Stroud Valley, seen clearly in the shape of Ebley and Stanley Mills below, and saw the end of the woollen industry in the five branch valleys.

It is from Selsley Common that you can detect another important boundary, this time military and from the Second World War: Stop-Line Green, often referred to as 'The Bristol Outer Defence Line', which was constructed during 1940. The line encircled Bristol, and its purpose was to protect the industry of that city and the port of Avonmouth from an inland attack from the east. It ran approximately 145km (90 miles), curving in a great loop from Highbridge on the Bristol Channel to Upper Framilode on the River Severn. The defence line was primarily an anti-tank obstacle and included 30km (18 miles) of dug anti-tank ditch, around 370 planned/built pillboxes and over 250 roadblocks. Pillboxes were built at regular intervals to command the line, in particular at the crossing points of roads and railways, which themselves would be set with concrete road and rail blocks. (See plate 21.)

This particular part of Gloucestershire was considered important, with many features that would have been very beneficial to an invading army, such as the navigable route along the River Severn to Tewkesbury, the Gloucester and Sharpness Canal as a vital supply route, the shallow beach/mudflats along the Severn which could have afforded easy landing access to an invading force, main railway routes, including the Severn Tunnel and Severn Railway Bridge, and several industrial manufacturing sites. The Stroudwater Canal was seen as another possible inland route.

As a result an anti-tank ditch was excavated from Malmesbury to Avening and the Nailsworth Gorge formed the section between Avening and Stroud. This natural defence line was reinforced on Minchinhampton Common by the numerous anti-aircraft trenches and pillboxes to deter gliders, especially. The Stroudwater Canal and River Frome became the final section from Stroud to Upper Framilode and the River Severn. The Stroudwater Canal around and below Stonehouse has many remaining pillboxes, and they are also to be found along the Arlingham bend of the River Severn.

SECTION 4

CEREMONY
SELSLEY COMMON TO DURSLEY

The route from King's Stanley, with its likely Roman temple, to Uley Bury Hill Fort is full of reference to ritual, belief and a continuity of worship from at least the Neolithic to the early medieval period. Why here? We may never know, but perhaps landscape is an important factor: one of the features that people comment about when on this part of the ridge are the enigmatic shapes

SECTION 4

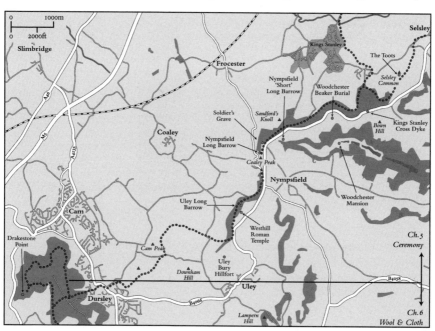

Ceremony: Selsley Common to Uley Bury.

of the hills, Cam Long Down, Peaked Down, and Downham Hill, immediately in front of the edge. On the Ordnance Survey map this is obvious, as the contours are so tight that they appear like the whorl prints of a thumb and fingers. You can see each from a distance. For example, conical Peaked Down can be identified easily from the train between Cheltenham and Bristol, from the M5 motorway and from the Forest of Dean. Across the River Severn is the Iron Age and Roman temple at Lydney dedicated to the god Nodens, a Celtic deity who was equated with Mars and Mercury. It has been suggested that the temple is connected with the phenomenon of the Severn Bore.

THE TOOTS (SO 827 032)

This long barrow is 72m (240ft) in length by 27.5m (90ft) wide and averaged 3m (10ft) in height; towards the west end it is 2m (6.5ft) high and at the east end 3.5m (11.5 ft) high. It is orientated east-north-east to west-south-west. There are no signs of a ditch and it has a large gash across the middle that makes it appear as two mounds, indicating that it has been opened in the past. In 1880, 'two hollowed stones from a burying place on Selsley Hill, and accompanying an interment' were exhibited at Stroud. If they were from this site,

as seems likely, they could have been the hollowed slabs of a port-hole entrance burial chamber. (See plate 22.)

52 'The Toots', Selsley Long Barrow. *Author's collection*

WOODCHESTER ROMAN VILLA (SO 839 031)

The villa at Woodchester lay in the valley just below Selsley Common. There are no visible remains of the palatial building, although some Roman brick is built into the ruins of the nearby church. The existence of the extraordinary mosaic pavements of the Woodchester Roman villa was first noted in 1693 and the pavements were uncovered by Edmund Brown in 1712 and 1722. During the remainder of the eighteenth century much damage was done by burials in the churchyard beneath which the remains lay. The villa was extensively cleared by the Rev Samuel Lysons in the 1790s when he located 65 rooms arranged around three rectilinear courtyards on substantially the same axis. This may reflect the formality of Great Witcombe villa, though Woodchester is larger. What is unique about this villa is a (possibly domed) room, 15m (50ft) square – the largest known in Britain – which contains the 'Great Pavement', featuring Orpheus as the roundel in the centre. Lysons thought the villa all of one build, but Giles Clarke, undertaking a key-hole excavation in 1973, suggested a scheme for the growth of the structure, with a range of rooms not dissimilar to a simple row villa in AD 79–117, followed by the centre and outer courts in the late second to early third centuries, and finally the inner courtyard in the first half of the fourth century.

There can be no doubt that some parts of the building were sumptuously decorated with marble sheathing, wall plaster and statues, and this has led to discussions of its function and ownership. To the present time no agricultural or industrial components have been discovered, although in the light of such limited excavation this claim might be presumptuous. There is every likelihood that Woodchester villa might be seen as being the home of a high-status political figure from another part of the Empire, connected perhaps with the government of the region.

SECTION 4

KING'S STANLEY CROSS DYKE (SO 818 021)

Just as at Randwick the neck of land was defined by a cross dyke, related to a long barrow and round barrows, so this similar feature cuts off a narrow neck of the long east-west ridge, which here forms part of the main escarpment of the Cotswolds. The earthwork is 219m (720ft) long, comprising a ditch on the west side, generally 10.6m (35ft) across, and a bank 15m (50ft) wide and up to 1m (3ft) high. As with the Randwick Cross Dyke there is no sign of an original entrance.

WOODCHESTER BEAKER BURIAL (SO 811 019)

A bowl barrow mound west of the cross dyke measuring about 25m (82ft) in diameter and up to 0.4m (1.3ft) high was surrounded by a quarry ditch which is no longer visible at ground level but survives as a buried feature about

3m (10ft) wide. In 1929, the mound was disturbed by workmen looking for road-building material and an almost complete Bronze Age beaker and human bones were found. The barrow was partially excavated by Elsie Clifford in 1949, who speculated that the area had first been cleared and the four pits dug into the underlying rock. These were then filled in with burnt material and a layer of earth was spread over the area, onto which a stone chamber was built measuring about 14.6m (48ft) in diameter and at least 1.3m (4.2ft) high. This cairn was then covered with an earthen mound. A fifth pit, 4m (13ft) long and 1.1m (3.6ft) wide, contained human or animal bones. She described this as a Roman grave inserted into the barrow.

NYMPSFIELD 'SHORT LONG BARROW' (SO 798 015)

The probable, pear-shaped, remains measure 32m (98 ft) in length by 25m (78ft) wide at the east end by 1.2m (31/2ft) high, orientated from east to west. It appears to be composed almost entirely of Oolitic slabs, and is much broader at the east, with a tail at the west end.

WOODCHESTER MANSION (SO 809 013)

Woodchester Mansion is a country house situated within Woodchester Park. The estate was purchased by William Leigh in 1845 from the Second Earl of Ducie. The Earl's house, Spring Park, had been built in the reign of George I but was in such poor repair that it was demolished. Augustus Pugin submitted designs for a new building and also a monastery, but these were not executed. Instead, Charles Hansom designed the monastery (completed in 1857 but demolished in 1970), and Benjamen Bucknall designed the house in Gothic style. Work commenced on the house in 1855 but stopped in 1869 and the building is still incomplete. The house has never been lived in, but a restoration of the grounds took place during the late 1990s. The house is a National Trust property.

SOLDIER'S GRAVE (SO 794 015)

A rather sad round cairn consisting entirely of stone of early Bronze Age (or possibly late Neolithic) date located in woodland c.200m (650ft) north of the Nympsfield long barrow on the escarpment edge overlooking the Vale of

53 Soldier's Grave near Nympsfield Long Barrow. *Author's collection*

54 Nympsfield Long Barrow. *Edward J. Burrow, 'Ancient Entrenchments and Camps of Gloucestershire', 1924, p. 15*

Berkeley. It was excavated in 1937, although by then it had been considerably disturbed, presumably by earlier unrecorded excavations. In 1937, it was measured at 17m (56ft) in diameter and 2.1m (7ft) high, although the previous unrecorded digging had left the centre resembling a large crater rather than a mound. A stone kerb also appears to have originally surrounded the foot of the mound. Beneath the centre was a rock-cut, boat-shaped pit lined with drystone walling, the pointed end facing south. The pit is presumed to have been covered originally by slabs, some being found in the nearby woodland. The pit was a maximum 3.3m (11ft) in length and 1.3m (4.5ft) wide, and was up to 1.1m (3.75ft) deep. It contained a large quantity of disturbed, disarticulated and fragmented human remains representing between twenty-eight and forty-four individuals, adults and children, males and females all being represented. Some animal bones (ox, pig and dog) were also in the pit, along with the skeletal remains of a further adult male, probably buried later.

NYMPSFIELD LONG BARROW (SO 793 013)

In the Coaley Peak viewing area, the Nympsfield long barrow is a trapezoidal Severn-Cotswold, transepted gallery grave, excavated by Professor Buckman in 1862, by Mrs Clifford in 1937 and by Alan Saville in 1974. It is orientated from east to west, with its maximum length and width *c.*27m (88.5ft) and 19.2m (63ft), although its edges have been denuded by ploughing. Excavations in 1974 before its restoration suggested that the mound would have been much higher at the east end, completely covering the chambers. The unroofed chambers are exposed and their stones stand up to 1.3m (4.2ft) high. The forecourt, a recess flanked by horns, is at the eastern end and leads into an entrance defined by two standing stones. Beyond this is the gallery or passage, now unroofed as the capstones were removed long ago, which allows an appreciation of the layout and design of the barrow. Stones sub-divided the passage and restricted access to two side chambers and an end chamber. On either side is a now in-filled 3m (10ft) wide ditch, from which material was originally taken to construct the barrow. In total, the excavations uncovered the remains of between twenty and thirty individuals, and evidence of a hearth and small pit suggesting that funerary rituals had been carried out when the barrow was in use. The forecourt was blocked with rubble and soil at the end of its life, preventing further access.

THE ULEY COMPLEX

Uley Long Barrow (SO 789 001)

Of all the long barrows along the route, Uley Long Barrow is the one that best gives an impression of what it would have been like when in use. The barrow gained the name 'Hetty Pegler's Tump' from two seventeenth-century owners of the field in which the barrow sits: Henry Pegler (d.1695) and his wife, Hester (d.1694). The mound consists of small stones and earth and is trapezoidal in plan, 36m (118ft) long and 26m (85ft) wide, orientated from north-east to south-west. It is flanked on either side by a ditch, now filled in, probably used for the construction of the monument. At the eastern end of the barrow there is a recess flanked by two horns to create a forecourt. The entrance to the mound is defined by two standing stones capped by a stone lintel and beyond the entrance is a stone gallery 10m (33ft) long and 1m (3.3ft) wide with overlapping slabs forming its roof. This leads to two pairs of side chambers and an end chamber. In 1821, an excavation was carried out by Dr Fry and T.J. Lloyd-Baker, who uncovered two human skeletons and the jaw bones of wild boar within the material blocking the entrance. (See plate 23.)

55 'No bones Eddie!' – the approach to Hetty Pegler's Tump. *Author's collection*

56 The porthole entrance to Hetty Pegler's Tump. *Author's collection*

57 Squeezing out of Hetty Pegler's Tump. *Author's collection*

Within the interior of the tomb thirteen human skeletons were revealed; six in the entrance passage (including two in a crouched position), four in the eastern side chamber (including one female skeleton and finds of animal teeth and Neolithic pottery), one in the western chamber and two in the north-eastern chamber. In addition, just below the surface of the mound, there was a single skeleton, believed to be an intrusive Romano-British burial, with three Constantinian (AD 312–337) coins. In 1854, an excavation by Dr J. Thurnham and Professor E.A. Freeman revealed more human remains, including nine human skulls, as well as animal teeth and boars' tusks. The barrow was reconstructed in 1854 by Dr John Thurnham and subsequently in 1871, 1891 and 1906. However, the north passage wall is a conjectural reconstruction as the original was destroyed by workmen searching for stone in 1821 and only the portals remain.

In 2008, Cotswold Archaeology examined the barrow in advance of repair work that was necessitated by subsidence in the earthen mound. The excavators inspected the large stones that make up the inside of the barrow by removing the mound above. However, the monument had been so thoroughly examined by the nineteenth-century excavations that no Neolithic deposits remained.

The continuity of this sacred space is seen in a round barrow just to the south at SO 787 001 – a similar relationship was seen at Belas Knap.

The West Hill Romano-British Temple (ST 789 997)

This site was first revealed by a pipe trench dug by the Severn and Trent Water Authority in the summer of 1976. A subsequent rescue excavation in 1977–79 by Ann Ellison revealed there was some evidence that the ditches of the substantial palisade of a late Iron Age shrine were aligned with those of a previous prehistoric structure, possibly Neolithic, which might have been silted up but was still visible. The late Iron Age shrine was situated on a high plateau overlooking the River Severn and facing east in dense woodland which was cleared away in the first centuries AD. The shrine itself comprised of postholes and beam slots of timber buildings in association with a large, square, ditched enclosure, and a smaller trapezoidal timber structure. Votive pits were found with human and infant burials, iron projectile heads, coins and partly complete fineware pottery vessels. Miniature martial objects such as bronze shields or weapons form significant parts of the assemblage, and many of these appear to have been deliberately broken prior to deposition in pits or dumps. The ritual use of animals implies that this was a regular method of religious appropriation, and the high number of bones related to goats leads to the proposition that the late Iron Age temple may have been dedicated to a horned god, which then led to the later interpretation of the deity as an equivalent to the Roman Mercury. What was unusual about the Uley square enclosure was that it seemed to have been constructed around a pit which may have contained a standing stone, timber post or living tree, and therefore the structure might have been open rather than roofed. This central feature was to remain important throughout the life of the subsequent Roman temple.

Probably in the early second century AD, the timber shrine was replaced on exactly the same alignment by a stone square structure similar to other known Romano-Celtic temples in Britain and in continental Europe. The foundations were fragmentary, because they had been disturbed by modifications in later periods, then raised to ground level, and subsequently damaged by several centuries of ploughing. However, it is possible that there were two major building phases, the first involving a slightly rectangular *cella* (the inner chamber of a temple in classical architecture) surrounded on three sides only by an *ambulatory* (a covered passage) of even width. The main entrance was probably located on the north-east side. No original floor levels survived and the only internal features that could have been related to the temple as it was primarily conceived were the central pit, which *may* have contained a lead tank or other water container, and a mortar base centrally positioned in the south-west ambulatory. This base *may* have been the remnant of a foundation for a plinth intended to support the major cult statue. The finding of the head of Mercury, which appears to have been deliberately removed and carefully deposited in a small pit, took place in the AD 380s during the dismantling and apparent desecration of the pagan temple. This may indicate a ritual that reflects the traditional respect for the head in Celtic religion and demonstrates continuity of worship from at least the late Iron Age, if not much earlier.

The temple lay at the centre of a large settlement with evidence of stone buildings and industrial activity. This field was formally known as Money Field and Samuel Rudder comments:

> This was certainly a Roman camp as I prove by the coins which have been found about it, the greater part being of the emperors Antoninus and Constantine of which Mr Small, late owner of the estate, has made a collection.

These temple precinct buildings have parallels at a number of similar shrines and presumably there would have been temporary booths or stalls set up for the selling of votive offerings, which were manufactured on site, to the pilgrims. There was a large structure close to the temple that may have acted as a guesthouse, but since Mercury had no healing attribution pilgrim accommodation with ritual baths was probably not needed. Subsequent buildings in the sub-Roman period consisted of a stone and timber building, and a small masonry building which may have been the foundations of a tower-like structure. Both were built immediately after the temple was demolished in *c.*AD 380 and can best be interpreted as successive Christian churches. Churches built on high points in the landscape are often constructed to counteract the pagan worship that had taken place, and might still continue to be undertaken, on the site.

58. Head of Mercury from Uley Temple.

The best evidence for the existence of Christianity comes from the temple in the form of a rectangular fragment of a copper alloy sheet found in a pit-like feature as a votive object. It would appear to be sheeting from a casket and may have belonged to people who felt the new faith was under imperial patronage and therefore very powerful. The four figured scenes on the embossed sheet could be interpreted as being two settings from the New Testament above two from the Old Testament. Those on the top might represent Christ and the Centurion and Christ healing the blind man. The lower scenes could be deciphered as Jonah and the sea monster and the sacrifice of Isaac. However, since many Roman religions share the same iconography and motifs, even in this case the interpretation is difficult. The folding and burial of this object might have been to 'kill' its significance, since it was probably a part of a casket that was no longer in use.

Uley Bury Hill Fort (Centred on ST 785 989)

Uley Bury, the most impressive of the Cotswold hill forts, is sub-rectangular and bivallate. It covers about 13ha (32 acres) and measures c.600m (656yds) by 200m (218yds) internally. It is generally flat, with the longer, parallel sides surviving, though the earthwork is mutilated in places by quarrying. It is likely that the defences were constructed by terracing of the already steep natural slopes. There are entrances at three corners of the fort; the main one is in the north, where a narrow neck of land joins the spur to the main mass of the Cotswolds. Outside the north entrance a series of banks and ditches have been

59 The rampart of Uley Bury hill fort. *Author's collection*

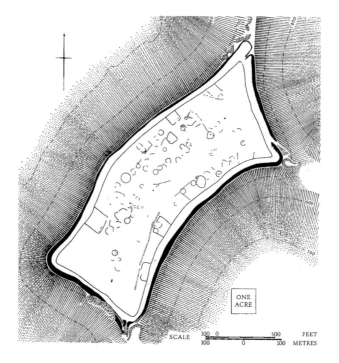

60 Aerial photographic evidence of settlement within Uley Bury hill fort. *J.N. Hampton and R. Palmer, 'Implications of aerial photography for archaeology',* Archaeological Journal, *Vol. 34, 1977, pp. 157–93*

noted but most of these have gone, and the surviving features appear natural. The remaining smaller entrances in the east and south cut through the outer rampart only. It is possible that there was another entrance gap, but this may be the result of later working. At the east corner, overlapping bank ends are associated with a hollow way, and at the damaged south entrance another is flanked on the west by a downward extension of the bank and by two partly artificial mounds. Trial excavations at the east entrance in 1976, prior to the laying of a pipeline through the fort, revealed a turf-and-timber entrance passage and Iron Age road metalling. Finds from the excavations included Iron Age pottery, a bronze ring-headed pin, a pennanular brooch, two shale amulets and a glass bead. During the laying of the pipe 'between the two entrances' a crouched burial, which is suggested as having been deposited during the Roman or sub-Roman periods, was located beneath two layers of limestone slabs. Cheltenham Museum houses an extensive collection of over 2,000 flint artefacts from Uley Bury, which include arrowheads, scrapers, knapping debris and eleven pieces from polished axe fragments, all of which suggest it was an important locale during the Neolithic period. The site has never been excavated internally, but aerial photographs show cropmarks of ditched enclosures inside the hill fort.

SECTION 5

WOOL AND CLOTH
DURSLEY TO WOTTON-UNDER-EDGE

This stretch of the Cotswold Way brings two of the themes together, as the towns at both ends of the section survived the demise of the wool trade and developed into cloth-manufacturing centres.

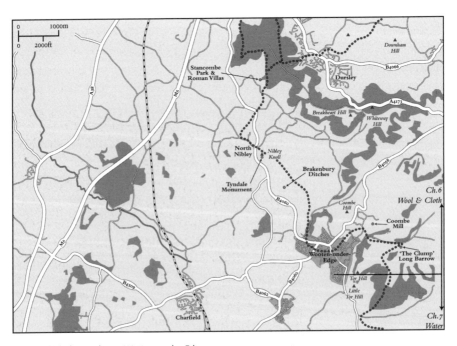

Wool and Cloth: Dursley to Wotton-under-Edge.

DURSLEY (CENTRED ON ST 757 981)

There are no traces of any prehistoric sites in Dursley, although worked flints have been found in Hermitage Wood above the town. Similarly, there is no evidence for a Roman-period presence, but there are significant sites of this date in the surrounding area such as at Uley Temple and the large settlement at Kingscote. The name 'Dursley' may have been derived from the Old English 'Deorsige's clearing', indicating Saxon origin. Dursley developed during the medieval period, acting as a market centre for the surrounding communities, but the form of the town has been significantly altered during the post-Second World War years.

The twelfth-century borough developed between the castle on the west and the church and market on the east. Long Street, along with Parsonage Street and Silver Street, formed the main structure of the medieval town. The back lanes (Water Street runs parallel to Long Street, and The Slade lies parallel to Parsonage Street and Silver Street) are likely to have formed an integral part of the medieval town plan. The church stands at the corner of Long Street and Silver Street. The earliest surviving stonework dates from the thirteenth century with fourteenth- to sixteenth-century additions. The junction of the three main streets forms a triangular area in which the market would have been held. A market cross stood in the centre of the area until it was replaced by the present market house in 1738.

It is thought that the medieval castle may have stood on the higher ground to the west of the settlement. In 1978 attempts to plant trees in the lawns of the Tabernacle Chapel, which was built in 1808 at the junction between Parsonage Street and Kingshill Road, were partially foiled by the presence of

61 Dursley Market House, built in 1738, which may have replaced an earlier market cross. *Countryside Agency: Nick Smith*

SECTION 5

large, dressed stones below turf level and thus may indicate the site of Dursley Castle. Dursley rose to prominence during the sixteenth century when it developed as one of the principal cloth-manufacturing centres along the Cotswold scarp.

The Cotswold Way enters Dursley through Long Street and many of the post-medieval mills and other works lay in this area outside the core of the settlement on the stream. Most have been demolished but evidence for the cloth trade has survived at Townsend's or Phelp's Mill, which stands at the top of Long Street. Weavers' houses would have been dotted throughout the town, including Nos. 1 and 19 Long Street, as working from home was common until the industrial developments of the nineteenth century encouraged mill owners and clothiers to concentrate their workforces in one place. The cloth industry continued to play an important role in the economy of the town through the seventeenth and eighteenth centuries and the resulting prosperity allowed the market cross to be replaced by the present market house in 1738. The ground floor of this building has an open arcade with stone columns, while a statue of Queen Anne sits in a niche on the first floor. In the ground-floor area were stalls on which boots, shoes, muslin, caps and other small items were displayed, while the butter market was held every Thursday on the first floor, which also doubled as the Town Hall.

During the early nineteenth century, the importance of the cloth trade began to decline and alternative industrial activities began to develop in its stead. However, the vast majority of buildings along the High Street, Long Street and Parsonage Street date to the eighteenth and nineteenth centuries, and many of these were associated with the clothing industry. Very little building took place in the Victorian period.

DRAKESTONE POINT (ST 736 980)

The earthworks at Drakestone Point occur on an almost level spur of Oolite and comprise about six sideways 'trenches' facing Stinchcombe Hill. At the north-east end two banks, with their central ditch, curve back on each side into the hillside; elsewhere the banks and ditches are straighter. The earthworks have been interpreted as a beacon communicating between the Iron Age forts of the neighbourhood, of which nine have been named, and the site of the castle built by Roger de Berkeley in 1153 after his loss of Berkeley Castle. These features bear no resemblance to a hill fort or castle and according to the Geological Survey are a series of natural 'gulls' produced when strong rocks such as the Oolitic limestone overlie weaker mudstone or clay-rich rocks.

62 Drakestone Beacon: not a hill fort, though from its postion it was felt that it should be. Burrow was very doubtful and illustrated from below. *Edward J. Burrow, 'Ancient Entrenchments and Camps of Gloucestershire', 1924, p. 69*

The tension between the strata produces joints or faults that develop parallel to the slope and may be seen as a step-like feature or linear depression at the ground surface. A small mound with a seat on top is possibly a round barrow about 7m (20ft) in diameter and 0.6.m (2ft) in height, with a central depression.

STANCOMBE PARK (ST 742 974)

The position of the spring line above Stancombe Park has resulted in the construction of two Roman villas and the nineteenth-century house and gardens. These three sequential displays of wealth are likely to reflect the situation at other sites along the route, with earlier structures having been destroyed by the later landscaping. The strip lynchets in a broken pattern east of Stancombe and about 270m (300yds) north of the larger villa probably represent 'Celtic' fields associated with the Roman buildings.

A small villa (ST 738 975) was discovered about 92m (100yds) from Stancombe Park House in 1819. Six rooms were revealed but no plan was discernible. The rooms were floored with Forest of Dean stone or cement and had plastered and painted walls. Finds included Samian pottery, rings, brooches and coins ranging from the time of Nero (54–68) to Constans (337–350). The un-coffined skeleton of a female, probably 18–24 years of age, was revealed 46m (50yds) from the building.

The larger Roman villa at Stancombe Park (ST 741 970) was discovered during the landscaping of the park and excavated *c.*1847 by P.B. Purnell, who reported the discovery of a room or passage 2.3m (7.5ft) wide with a plain mosaic pavement. A suite of rooms heated by hypocaust was found, including a large apartment thought to be the *atrium* (the formal, central hall open to the air and often holding a small pool to collect rain) containing the bases of two rows of stone columns. Many walls adjacent to Stancombe Park are built wholly or in part of re-used large squared blocks of Oolite and flagstones of Pennant and Old Red Sandstone from the Forest of Dean stone which could have come from the villa.

STANCOMBE PARK MANSION (ST 738 974)

A fire destroyed the original mansion in 1840 and the present classical-looking house dates from 1880. A 'Secret Garden', the inspiration of the Reverend David Purnell-Edwards, was created around 1815 using a team of soldiers back from the Napoleonic Wars who had recently disbanded at Avonmouth. The Reverend embarked on the concept of an idealised walk around a 0.8ha (2 acres) lake that would encapsulate all the important civilisations: Chinese, Egyptian and Greek architectural styles led to a small Doric temple. He also devised a series of tunnels to reach the garden, and tradition has it that he created them for his love trysts with a beautiful local gypsy. The tunnels were supposed to be too narrow for his wife, a portly lady with a large dowry, to pass through; she must have been quite some size, as the width of the tunnels is at least 3ft! The temple was thoroughly restored by English Heritage in 1996 and is now used, appropriately, as a 'romantic getaway' for holidays and events.

NORTH NIBLEY (ST 730 960)

A battle, said to be the last fought in England between two private armies, took place at Nibley Green on 20 March 1470 between the followers of Lord Lisle and those of William, Twelfth Lord Berkeley. About 1,000 men were engaged and 150 slain, including Lord Lisle himself. The 150 skeletons found in a communal grave close to Nibley church in Victorian times are thought to be those of the casualties of this battle.

TYNDALE MONUMENT (ST 743 958)

This tower, 34m (111ft) high, was 'Erected AD 1866 in grateful remembrance of William Tyndale, translator of the English Bible which first caused the New Testament to be printed in the mother tongue of his country-men; born near this spot, he suffered martyrdom at Vilvorde in Flanders on 6th October 1536'. Tyndale was born in Nibley in 1484.

63 The Tyndale Monument, celebrating the life of William Tyndale, who translated the Bible into English. *Author's collection*

BRACKENBURY DITCHES (ST 747 948)

This is a roughly triangular, possibly unfinished, Iron Age promontory fort, which occupies the south-west end of a steep-sided spur. It appears to be of two-phase construction: it is univallate except in the north-east, where an outer rampart of bank and ditch cuts the spur from north-west to the south-east; together the two defences enclose about 3.2ha (8 acres). The outer rampart runs parallel to the Cotswold Way path and, now cleared of woodland, its ditch can be seen as being 6m (20ft) wide and 1.2m (4ft) deep, fronting a bank 7.5m (25ft) wide and 1.5m (5ft) high. There is a gap at the south end which leads into the space between the two sets of defences and then along the scarp edge and into the inner defences through an entrance halfway on their south-eastern bank. There is also a hollow way up the scarp into this entrance. The inner defences enclose about 2ha (5 acres), and on the north-west and south-east sides, they follow the edge of the spur. On the north-east, the inner defences faced the outer work and consisted of a rampart 15.2m (50ft) wide and 3.5m (10ft) high and an external ditch 14m (45ft) wide and 2.4m (8ft) deep. Several low causeways in ditch of the inner defences suggest that it was either poorly completed or unfinished, and this perhaps indicates that the outer work is the earlier of the two.

64 Brackenbury Ditches: the outer rampart being cleared of trees and undergrowth. *Author's collection*

TUMULUS (ST 752 937)

A doubtful round barrow about 18.2m (60ft) in diameter and 0.6m (2ft) high sits on the extreme point of Wotton Hill. It has been planted with trees and a modern wall has been built round them. The clump of trees was first planted here in 1815 to commemorate the Battle of Trafalgar. In 1887 the site was used for a beacon during Queen Victoria's Jubilee and the wall was erected at the end of the Crimean war. The present trees were planted in 1952.

WOTTON-UNDER-EDGE (CENTRED ON ST 756 933)

Wotton-under-Edge lies at the point where the steep embayments of the Cotswold escarpment give way to a gentler landscape, where the land falls to the wide valley of the Severn. Its name seems to derive from 'farmstead in the wood under the Cotswold Edge' and this describes its location perfectly, lying partly on a shelf sheltered from the north winds and partly in one of the combes. There is little evidence for prehistoric or Roman activity in the area and it seems that Cotswold wool was the basis of its early development. The monks of Kingswood Abbey, a Cistercian foundation which stood about 2.5km (1.5 miles) to the south-east and whose sixteenth-century gatehouse still survives (ST 747 920), were known to be expert sheep farmers and also had connections to Italian and Flemish wool buyers who came to England every summer. It is therefore likely that much of the wool from the Kingswood flocks was sold through the market at Wotton. The trade in raw wool was developed into the manufacture of cloth as the town was ideally located for its production, having fast-flowing streams for powering fulling mills, and for the dyeing process, while fuller's earth could be dug locally and wool was widely available.

Dropping down to just below the escarpment, the Cotswold Way enters Wotton through the core of the thirteenth-century Borough. Bradley Street, High Street and Long Street form the main east–west axis of a simple grid plan, with Haw Street, Bear Street and Orchard Street running north–south at right angles to them, encompassing an area of almost 24ha (60 acres). Until the later nineteenth century, Gloucester Street was known as Back Street or Back Lane, suggesting that it marked the northern extent of the Borough.

The thirteenth-century marketplace was laid out at the bottom of Market Street, to the south of the High Street, in the area known as The Chipping, which would originally have had the form of a large square area at the centre of which stood the market hall. Its location to the south of the High Street is unusual, as it does not lie on any of the main routes through the settlement. This may be related to the volume of produce, especially wool, which was traded through the town during the later medieval period, and which required a separate trading area. By the post-medieval period the market square contained the butchers' shambles at its southern end, the fishmongers' stalls stood at the northern end of this area, close to the Swan Inn, and a Cheese Cross is also known to have stood in the marketplace under some form of roofed structure, although its exact location is unknown. The annual fairs were held outside the borough in the area immediately south of The Chipping known as the Green Chipping (now a car park). In this area wooden stalls were set up in streets, and each merchant paid a fee to the lord of the manor for the use of a booth. During the later medieval and post-medieval periods, the market outgrew The Chipping, possibly due to much of the open area being in-filled with permanent buildings instead of temporary stalls, and the Green Chipping was brought into use as a market also.

The district known as Old Town, which includes much of the area around the church and manor house, is named after the earliest part of the town onto which the Borough was added in the mid-thirteenth century. This would explain both the isolation of the church and manor from the commercial heart of the settlement, and the marked contrast between the broad, roughly parallel streets of the Borough and the knot of narrow streets around the church and

SECTION 5

Dyer's Brook. Most of the fabric of the present church dates to the thirteenth century, although there have been a number of later additions and alterations. The medieval manor house is thought to have stood to the east of the church, within its own enclosure and with a gatehouse at the entrance to Manor Lane.

An area on the southern side of Gloucester Street – called Rack Close on the tithe map of 1839, and which also formed part of Old Town – is thought to have been set aside for drying and stretching woven cloth from the town mills. The mills in the Old Town area were steam-driven and, therefore, did not need to be sited in the valley. The Old Town Weaving Factory was an early steam mill, with three storeys in local stone and a slate roof. It is now occupied by the Cotswold Book Room, at 26 Long Street. The Old Town Mill, just to the east of the Catholic church on Old Town, has been converted to housing and heavily modified, but the range of two- and three-storeyed buildings still reflects the frontage of the steam-powered mill which is likely to have originated during the earlier medieval period. Close to the library was Steep Mill, one of the first in the county to be built wholly as a steam mill and away from the valley bottom. In 1830 the property consisted of a large building of four storeys used for counting houses, wool lofts, cloth, and yarn and pressing rooms; an engine house was attached to the mill and a stream ran behind it. There were also an air stove, two cottages for workmen, a blacksmiths and carpenters' shops and other buildings well adapted for machinery or warehouses.

Wotton survived the changes to the industry in the later fifteenth and sixteenth centuries, unlike many other Cotswold wool towns, and continued to flourish into the nineteenth century, until increased mechanisation and competition from new markets caused its decline. Within the area of the Borough most development took the form of infilling of vacant plots, and the re-fronting or rebuilding of many of the older houses and structures in the Georgian style.

DYEHOUSE MILL (ST 763 936)

The route of the Cotswold Way follows Dyer's Brook, which once powered the mills every quarter of a mile in the seventeenth and eighteenth centuries, and joins the Little Avon at Kingswood. Dyehouse Mill was built in the nineteenth century and cloth was being produce at the site in 1830. When the cloth industry in Wotton collapsed Dyehouse Mill became solely a dyeworks. The mill is a single-storey building which formerly had a glass roof on its north-facing side. Adjacent to the mill is an older mill house.

COMBE MILL (ST 770 939)

The site contains a three-storeyed former mill building with a gabled roof. Probably built in the early or mid-nineteenth century, the building has now been converted to housing. The building is rendered and has been heavily modified. The mill lakes, covering 2.8ha (7 acres), still exist.

LONG BARROW (ST 775 932)

A probable long barrow at Blackquarries Hill, known locally as 'The Clump', the barrow is 40m (130ft) long by 18.2m (60ft) wide by 1.5m (5ft) high, orientated from north-east to south-west. It is now planted with trees and enclosed by a modern wall. There is a local tradition of soldiers being buried here, but the site is thought to be the possible confused remains of quarrying for 'tilestone'.

SECTION 5

SECTION 6

WATER
WOTTON-UNDER-EDGE TO LANSDOWN

As the Cotswold Way runs towards Tormarton you might find that the view becomes less relentlessly spectacular and more comfortably human in scale. So far the Cotswold Way has not passed through many villages and has rarely dropped below the spring line. This section of the route descends below the scarp and uses medieval, or older, footpaths that linked small communities below. As you will experience, each village is unique and so the reasons for its development are complex, but the spring line was *the* vital factor in location and survival. The Oolitic limestones are permeable and well jointed, and water runs through them down to the impermeable Upper Lias sands and clays. Wherever the escarpment cuts through this junction a spring is formed. However, because the limestones do allow so much water through them, there can be seasonal variation in the discharge of the springs, so it is not usual in a hot summer to see springs at a higher level dry up while those further down the slope are still active. (See plate 25.)

The villages currently existing along the route are known to have been there at least since early medieval times when about 95 per cent of the population of England was still rural, and probably many of them were in existence hundreds of years before that. The most common archaeological monuments along the route are churches and burial grounds, which needed ritually symbolic water for baptisms. Churches are usually found close to the manor house, which often possessed such elements as a farm, barns, dovecot and fishponds in the core of the village. Frequently, smaller village buildings are in evidence in the village centre, such as a pound for straying animals and perhaps a village cross or similar point of assembly. There are very few villages that are clustered in a

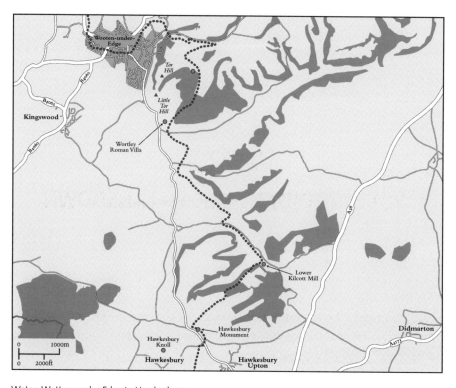

Water: Wotton-under-Edge to Hawkesbury.

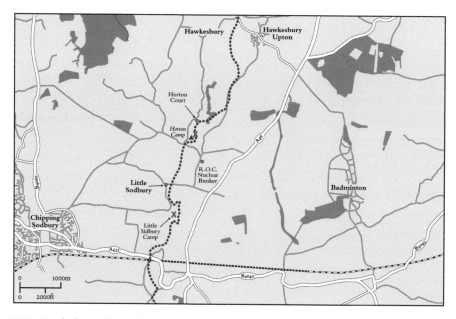

Water: Hawkesbury to Little Sodbury.

tight group around the church as the hilly nature of the landscape suggests that they developed along the spring line, which resulted in them being strung out along a road as at Old Sodbury. Some villages are dispersed with only a small settlement around the church, as at Hawkesbury Upton, where the village was moved up the hill deliberately to attract trade. This is also the case with the development of country houses such as Horton Court, Dyrham Park and Doddington House, with the village dispersed around the parish away from the 'Big House'.

It is increasingly being realised that village plans can alter over centuries, and even churches, the most stable element of the community, may be replaced on other sites within the village. Some villages, such as Tormarton and Hinton, have shrunk and the earthworks of previous house platforms ('tofts') within the land around them ('crofts') can be seen on the outskirts of the present settlement.

Also situated along the spring line are a number of Roman villas, which were individual expressions of wealth and taste usually associated with a rural estate, and reflect the attitudes and the status of the owners. On a continuum from small house to palatial complex, the defining features are the presence, number and quality of hypocausts, mosaics and architectural ornamentation such as painted plaster. The growing taste for Roman styles and building techniques would also be seen in the number of rooms, and especially the presence of at least one bathhouse. What is rarely explored are ornamental gardens, which have been detected in villas where the area available for excavation has been large enough to locate them.

South of Wotton-under-Edge are a large number of country houses on, or near, the sites of Roman villas (as at Stancombe, through which you have already passed). This is not entirely coincidental as the geological environment suited both types of house, with shelter from the north and east winds, plentiful wood as fuel for the heating systems, and sources of water valuable in the country house for filling ornamental lakes. There are great similarities between the 'English Country House' and Romano-British villas – they are displays of wealth and power, probably to impress the neighbours, built up over many generations, which reflect the economic and political climate of the times and evolved over many hundreds of years. Country houses of both periods are an indigenous adaption of Continental forms of architecture and the affinity felt between those living in classically designed houses and their Roman forebears was often seen in excavations of villas which were discovered when landscaping parks.

WORTLEY THATCHED COTTAGE ROMAN 'VILLA' (ST 769 918)

Few Roman structures along the Cotswold Way have undergone substantial excavation in the past fifty years, though one that has is at Wortley. As is often the case, the 'villa' was discovered by accident by the then landowner digging a hole for a fencepost and coming up with a piece of mosaic flooring and pieces of painted wall plaster. Some local enthusiasts opened a trench which revealed the badly damaged *pilae* (pillars holding up the floor) of a hypocaust system of parts of two rooms of a bathhouse, together with considerable quantities of painted, wall plaster, *tesserae* (the small stones that make up a mosaic) and *tegulae* (roof tile), some pottery and bone. In 1983 the site was taken over by the University of Keele as a training excavation directed by David Wilson (to whom I am indebted for this account). (See plate 24.)

The uniqueness of the Wortley site lies in two of its structures: its cellar and its bathhouse. Cellars on Romano-British sites are commonly seen as storage areas; they are relatively rare in Roman Britain, and their construction is mainly restricted to the period AD 70–155. But the cellar at Wortley was, in origin, not a simple storage facility, but an underground cult room. The evidence for this special use is fourfold: first, the walls had been decorated by coloured painting rather than the plain whitewash of a storage room; second, the southern wall had niches in it which may have held cult images; third, the cellar had two splay windows in its western wall, not on its own an indicator of a cult room, but significant when considered in conjunction with the other evidence; fourth, there is association of the cellar with water. This latter was strikingly evidenced by a cruciform channel system beneath the cellar's concrete floor, running from the central point of the floor to the west, east and south, with the beginning of a fourth channel running northwards under the half of the cellar not available for excavation.

SECTION 6

65 Wortley Roman 'Villa':
Capstoned channels
under floor of cellar.
David Wilson

66 Wortley Roman 'Villa': Capstones on southern channel under floor of cellar. *David Wilson*

67 Wortley Roman 'Villa': Stone lintel supporting western wall over channel in cellar, with folded lead sheet in situ. *David Wilson*

Each of these channels was covered by capstones mortared onto the stone edges of the channels. The most surprising aspect, however, was that all three complete channels ran beneath the walls of the cellar, under rough stone lintels, but ended at the outer limits of the walls. Consequently, they were not part of any drainage system, but were associated solely with the cellar. The function of these channels is still not certain but two large, folded pieces of lead found in the western channel may have formed the lining for a font-like feature set within a hole found in the centre of the concrete floor, immediately above the junction of the channels. This 'font' may have contained water brought up by seepage via the channels, depending on the water table at the time, or it may have been used to receive libations, which would then run into the channels. No parallel has been noted in either Britain or abroad for these channels.

The first striking thing about the bathhouse was its size: almost 14m (48ft) in length and comprising six areas, ranging from a hot room to a latrine. The *natatarium* or swimming pool in the bathhouse is some 13.7m (45ft) long and 2.2m (7.2ft) wide internally, and extremely rare outside of large urban sites; it would seem to be the largest of any known on a rural site. Another rare, if not unique, aspect of the pool was that there was no evidence of any non-porous

68 Wortley Roman 'Villa': Natatarium showing Roman robbing and the stone base with cross-wall, which supported the postulated lead tank. *David Wilson*

lining to the surface or the walls, and so it seems that it took the form of a large lead tank sitting upon a pitched stone surface. The inner faces of the two north–south walls were badly damaged, suggesting the vigorous removal of such a tank. Interestingly, the cold plunge bath showed a similar lack of non-porous lining to its floor and what remained of its walls, again pointing to the use of lead to provide a 'tank'.

The excavators are still debating the function of the site, but it seems very likely that it was a cult 'centre' with, perhaps, accommodation for people visiting it. On the other hand, it might have been a more 'private' religious complex associated with an adjacent 'villa', a possibility suggested by magnetic suscepti-bility tests which indicate buildings (of unknown date) in an adjacent field.

LOWER KILCOTT MILL (ST 786 893)

There are a number of mills in the charming valley of the Kilcott Brook, the most complete being Lower Killcott Mill, a small farm water mill which has been restored to working order. It was mentioned in Domesday Book of 1086 and was probably in existence previous to that. The present building dates partially from 1655 and the mill house that stands close by was built a little later in 1677. Water comes from Kilcott Brook via a short penstock, a chan-nel bringing water from the head gates to a water wheel, to the 5.5m (18ft) diameter pitchback wheel (an overshot wheel where the water goes down behind it) about 4.2m (14ft) in diameter and 0.9m (3ft) wide, with an unusual combination of cast-iron and wrought-iron spokes. The wheel drives a single set of stones. The tailrace empties through a 182m (100yd) tunnel that rejoins the stream after running under the mill house. Restoration work included

SECTION 6

dredging the millpond and dam, and repairing the wheel, gates and tunnels. It began a new working life in 1977.

HAWKESBURY KNOLL (ST 768 872)

A long barrow is situated upon the summit and orientated south-east to north-west, with the wider and higher end to the north, but with no traces of side ditches. This northern end of the barrow is most probably a medieval or post-medieval extractive pit, for which there is an associated spread of spoil extending downslope. It is now about 20m (66ft) in length measured along the spine.

LORD ROBERT SOMERSET MEMORIAL TOWER (HAWKESBURY MONUMENT) (ST 772 876)

This tower, approximately 30m (100ft) high, was built in 1846 by local freemasons to commemorate Lord Robert Edward Somerset, who was a general at Waterloo and died in 1842.

HAWKESBURY (CENTRED ON ST 768 870) AND HAWKESBURY UPTON (CENTRED ON ST 781 870)

The church of St Mary at Hawkesbury (ST 768 870) is said to date from 680, when a college for secular canons was founded there by Oswald of Northumbria, nephew of King Ethelred (the Unready). The only visible Saxon work remaining is the base of one of the shafts, or possibly the bases of both shafts, of the Norman north doorway and an interlaced cross-shaft fragment built into the fifteenth-century pulpit. The foundations of a wall, possibly dating from the seventh century, were found beneath the west end of the nave during alterations to the church in 1882–85, but are not exposed to view. The church also has a Norman north doorway, a fifteenth-century nave and a massive west tower of the same date. It is likely that the high quality of the church was related to its being in the ownership of the Abbot of Pershore.

The traces of the Manor House (ST 769 870), demolished in the early nineteenth century, lie just to the north of Hawkesbury parish church with part of the northern, southern and western walls represented by linear banks, suggesting a north–south oriented building which measured 40m (131ft) long by 21m

(69ft) wide, with an outer boundary ditch. The Manor House is of unknown date, but was probably built after the dissolution of the Abbey of Pershore in 1539. Three large medieval fish ponds are located behind Church Farm. North and south of it are a series of platforms, which have been identified as formal garden terrace features, but are more likely to be the sites of former cottages which may form evidence for an area of a shrunken village depopulated for the construction of the manor or due to the laying out a new settlement on the plateau above.

In 1252 the Abbot of Pershore was granted the right to hold a weekly market or fair on his manor at Hawkesbury; this grant seems to have been the spur to lay out a new settlement adjacent to the existing hamlet of Upton. Hawkesbury Upton's long, narrow burgage plots were laid out on either side of the High Street and Park Street, their slightly curved shape suggesting that they were placed directly on the existing pattern of medieval field strips. Traces of field boundaries to the north and south of the High Street have tentatively been identified as the possible extent of the planned town area.

The presence of a 'Bath Lane' near Hawkesbury Upton, the line of which continues along the escarpment as Highfield Lane and New Tyning Lane and then on the A46, a recognised Roman road to Bath, suggests that the Cotswold Way has become more than a local 'insider' route.

HORTON COURT (ST 766 850)

The north wing of Horton Court dates from the twelfth century and is one of the very few examples of Norman unfortified domestic buildings remaining in England. The rest of the house is mainly sixteenth-century Tudor Gothic, built in 1521. Horton Court is surrounded by earthwork remains of a medieval landscape comprising three areas of house platforms east of the Court, a group of earthworks west and a further four irregular platforms up to 1.5m (5ft) high further west with evidence of hollow ways. The date of desertion is unclear, but it may have been caused by a change in the road network. There are also four fishponds, a hunting park and a rabbit warren. The church of St James (ST 766 850) was built in the fourteenth century on the site of a Norman church and was altered in the fifteenth and sixteenth centuries, and restored in 1865. Each of these stages probably represents the accumulation of wealth by consecutive owners.

Horton Camp. 9 acres
Ed.J.Burrow.1914.

69 Horton Camp. *Edward J. Burrow, 'Ancient Entrenchments and Camps of Gloucestershire',
1924, p. 79*

HORTON CAMP (ST 764 843)

This promontory fort of about 2ha (9 acres) has a single bank and ditch on
its north and east sides. The bank is 12m (40ft) wide by 3.5m (11ft) high,
4.8m (16ft) tall in places, and the ditch is traceable as a band of dark, stoneless
ploughed soil 7.5m (25ft) wide. There are natural defences on the other two
sides, but the remains of a rampart 0.6m (2ft) high extend for a short distance
along the southern side where the natural slopes are weak. The position of
the entrance is uncertain but was possibly on the north side. Exposed parts of
the rampart show fire-reddened limestone on the outer face, midway along
its length.

THE SITE OF A ROYAL OBSERVER CORPS
MONITORING POST (ST 766 838)

Just south of New Tyning Lane junction with Horton Hill is a complete
underground structure with steps up to its main hatch and two air purifiers in
its roof. It was built as part of an extensive network of posts designed to confirm and report hostile aircraft and nuclear attacks on the United Kingdom.
It was opened during May 1960 and closed in September 1991. The facility is
similar to the one at Broadway Tower (SP 114 361).

70 Horton nuclear bunker. *Author's collection*

LITTLE SODBURY (CENTRED ON ST 759 833)

St Adeline's church (the only dedication known to this saint) may look medieval, but it was built in 1859 partly from materials of an earlier one which stood behind the manor house. The church was very small, having only nave and one aisle, and today nothing remains of the original except for the south doorway, which can be seen in a wood below the farm at the hill fort.

The Manor House dates from the early fifteenth century. It was altered and extended in the late fifteenth or early sixteenth century, and early to mid-seventeenth century. It was also partly restored in the early eighteenth century after a storm, and extensively restored *c.*1913–1920. Despite the Manor House being fifteenth century and later, and the adjacent remains of the medieval church, there is no ground evidence of an associated village settlement.

To the west, north and east of the Manor House and occupying 22ha (54 acres) are a series of linear earthworks, of varying length and preservation but all constructed by mounding up soil, mostly between parallel ditches. These typically low, flat-topped mounds comprise a dozen or so in each group, averaging 30m (98ft) long and 6m (20ft) wide in most cases, with side ditches 2m (6.5ft) wide which can be traced around one or both ends. These types of earthworks are identified as 'pillow mounds', artificial warrens for rabbits, although they have often been misinterpreted as long or round barrows or, in the case of Witts, as the burials of Roman soldiers associated with the hill fort above. The rabbit was introduced into England, probably from Iberia, by the Normans for its fur and meat, but most pillow mounds are of post-medieval origin, many functioning up until the early eighteenth century, providing masses of cheap meat (they also produced rabbit pelts for trimming and varnishing in the manufacture of top hats). Sometimes pillow mounds had an internal structure of tunnels that provided artificial runs and burrows and exits which were often drilled from

SECTION 6

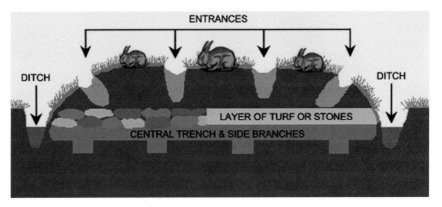

71 Cross-section of a typical pillow mound. *http://www.legendarydartmoor.co.uk/rabb_warr.htm*

the top as boreholes. On these sites there are no signs of either feature. Warrens, sometimes of considerable size as at Little Sodbury, boasted extensive banks to enclose the pillow mounds and other features, including vermin traps and pit-falls for catching the rabbits. The close proximity to the manor house suggests that the warren was under private rather than common ownership, and as they are all constructed over the broad ridge and furrow it is likely that they date from the sixteenth to seventeenth centuries.

LITTLE SODBURY CAMP (ST 761 825)

This Iron Age hill fort is situated near the western edge of a plateau at 186m (600ft), with the interior being perceptibly higher than the surrounding area. The fort is under permanent pasture, though traces of narrow ridge and furrow are visible in the southern half. The low bank across the interior is of uncertain origin, but most probably indicates the medieval parish boundary. Except on the west, where the natural slope is moderately steep, the monu-ment is bivallate, comprising two widely spaced ramparts enclosing an inner area of 4.5 ha (1 acre). The inner rampart is set along the edges of a slight rise on the north, east and south, where it is about 10.6m (35ft) wide, and rises 2.1m (7ft) above the interior, but along the scarp edge on the west it is lower. The ditch, 9m (30ft) wide and 2.1m (7ft) deep on the plateau, drops round the north corner to follow a natural terrace below the scarp edge for about 121m (400ft) where a low bank accompanies it. A steep and deep cleft midway along the west seems to be a constructional feature rather than worn through the rampart, but it is uncertain whether this is original, for agricultural use, or leading down to a spring. At the entrance, in the middle of the east side, the staggered ends of the rampart contain fire-reddened limestone.

72 Sodbury Camp. *Edward J. Burrow, 'Ancient Entrenchments and Camps of Gloucestershire', 1924, p. 105*

There is an inter space from 12m (39ft) to 20m (65ft) between the inner rampart and the outer one which terminates to the north and south at the escarpment edge. The purpose of this flat area might have been as a place to fold animals away from predators at night. Around the north, the outer rampart is at best 2m (6.5ft) high and appears to consist of earth scraped up from over a wide area. Along the east side, between the irregularly dumped rampart and an almost flat-bottomed shallow ditch, there is a berm, and this is still apparent at the entrance terminals. Around the south-east corner and on part of the south side the ditch seems to have been partly ploughed in, but there is a distinct termination just west of the corner, beyond which the outer rampart appears to be constructed from scrape-up material. All of this evidence points to the hill fort being left unfinished. (See plate 26.)

Part of a saddle quern was found inside the fort in 1958 and Roman coins, ranging from Gallienus (AD 218–268) to Constantius II (AD 317–361), have been found within it, or in the vicinity.

Witts, in 1883, thought Sodbury Camp the 'most perfect Roman Camp in the County of Gloucestershire'. This is understandable considering it is of typical Roman 'playing-card' shape, which produces a large and efficient space, and *appeared* to be set within an irregularly shaped, earlier Iron Age hill fort. The well-known 'type-site' for this arrangement was at Hod Hill in Dorset where the Roman engineers had used the corner of a rectangular Iron Age fort for a double-ditched military base of their own and it is highly likely that Witts would have been aware of this.

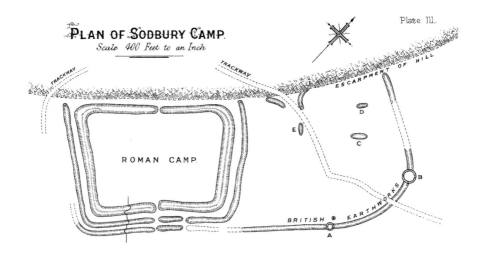

73 Plan of Sodbury Camp by Witts. He thought that the rectangular area was a Roman fort inside Iron Age defences. It is more likely that the rectangular feature is the Iron Age hill fort, the other 'defences' being related to the pillow mounds (not Roman soldiers' graves!) below. The 'towers' were probably tree rings. TBAS, *Vol. 8, 1883–84, pp. 74–8*

There is evidence of a very low bank marked on the Ordnance Survey map running from the north-east corner of the outer rampart and curving inward towards the edge of the escarpment. Although it has largely been ploughed out beyond the farm track, as late as 1976 it was prominent in the landscape as a linear bank, 100m (328ft) long, 14m (45 ft) wide and 0.8m (2.5ft) high with a ditch 8.5m (28ft) wide on its inner, western, side. Witts suggested that it turned west and onto the escarpment where it ended although there was no trace of this in the 1970s. From this he concluded that this linear ditch was that of a 'British' fort within which the Romans constructed their military post. However, the earthwork was much more likely to be related to the rabbit warrens below. The idea of the Sodbury fort being Roman was certainly current as late as the 1930s, when it was seen as a fort on a secondary road between Cirencester and Bath

DODINGTON HOUSE (ST 752 799)

The Codrington family acquired this estate in the late sixteenth century, when there was a large gabled Elizabethan house which had been constructed *c.* 1560 adjoining a church. In the eighteenth century, the family became wealthy from sugar plantations in the West Indies and undertook work on the estate.

The original house at Dodington Park was rebuilt 1796–1816 as a great classical mansion by James Wyatt, with finely cut and squared limestone and a slate and copper roof in a Roman classical style.

The grounds of 240ha (593 acres) were laid out around 1764 by Capability Brown as an idealised romantic landscape, containing classical garden buildings and lodges, summer houses and two irregular lakes linked by serpentine aqueduct and castellated Gothic cascade. In the 1930s terraced flower gardens with a fountain, a perimeter tree belt and woodlands were added. The lakes are fed by the River Frome, which rises on the spring line in the park and is crossed before leaving the park. Roman villa remains have been found at Dodington, 'within two miles of the very perfect Roman camp at Sodbury' possibly within the park.

TORMARTON VILLAGE SHRINKAGE (ST 770 788)

The church of St Mary, which has Norman beginnings and later alterations and additions, was at the centre of a medieval village, which has shrunk on its north and north-east sides. This area of desertion is large, 3.75ha (9.2 acres), and is occupied by earthworks which are rectangular enclosures, approximately 40m (131ft) by 30m (98ft), made up of rubble of up to 0.3m (1ft). It is likely that they represent the 'tofts', the land around the houses or 'crofts', which was used for growing vegetables. The 'crofts' are represented by small rectangular platforms and depressions. The whole area has been robbed of the stone from the buildings and rubbish tipped from elsewhere, resulting in the remains of the structures being very confused. This may also be the reason why no original trackways between the tofts and the church are now visible.

West Littleton Down 'Celtic' fields (Centred on ST 773 772 on 'access land')

These comprise a complicated system of low banks covering 20.2ha (50 acres), most of them running parallel to the boundaries of the Down. They are difficult to trace at close quarters – much of the remains have been ploughed out and partly obscured by ridge and furrow – but they are evident at a distance and from the air. Where banks do survive they are generally much spread by ploughing and are up to 0.7m high. However some of the earthworks may originate in a Second World War bombing decoy at West Littleton that was built to deflect enemy bombing from Royal Air Force Colerne airfield. This was a 'Q-type' night decoy, which displayed a series of lights to simulate an active airfield. It is recorded as being in use from 1941 to 1942.

SECTION 6

West Littleton Down 'round barrow' (ST 769 773)

Little is known about this feature, but it is recorded on pre–Second World War Ordnance Survey maps and it has been suggested that it is related to the field system.

Bronze Age Burials (ST 767 767)

In 1968, during the insertion of a gas pipeline at West Littleton Down, the skeletons of three men were found, two of them displaying combat wounds with points of late–middle Bronze Age spearheads buried in them. A further hole was visible in one of the men's skulls and a bronze spearhead transfixed his spine. In 1999 and 2000, further excavation work took place on the site and found that the bodies had been thrown into part of a 60m-long (196ft-long) ditch, probably a boundary. Following the study of the skeletal remains, it now appears that five young men were deposited in the ditch. Although only two of the bodies displayed signs of violence, the fact that they had all been buried in the same place, and by a quick filling-in of the ditch, would indicate that they had all been killed in a single episode, possibly a boundary dispute.

DYRHAM CAMP (ST 741 767)

Dyrham Camp, otherwise known as Hinton Hill Fort, is an unexcavated univallate fort. The end of the south-west facing spur is isolated by the eastern rampart and outer ditch, thus protecting an area of about 7.2ha (18 acres). Basically triangular in shape, it is cut into two by the little road up the hillside from the village of Hinton below. The unploughed southern part of the rampart is about 10.6m (35ft) wide, rises 2.4m (8ft) above the interior and 4m (13ft) above the bottom of the ditch, which is 6m (20ft) wide. The southern side of the spur has been scarped but the steepness of this side requires little artificial defence, although there are numerous quarry diggings throughout this area and no trace of a rampart. The entrance was presumably on the east at the point utilised by the present road.

Although there is little known about the archaeology of this site as it has never been excavated, it has a significance and importance in history much greater than its remains would suggest. Under the year 577 the *Anglo-Saxon Chronicle*, which was assembled on the orders of King Alfred the Great in approximately AD 890 as the official history of the West Mercian lineage, states:

> Cuthwine and Ceawlin (West Saxons) fought with the Britons at a place called Deorham and killed three kings, Coinmail, Condidan and Farinmail and took three 'chesters', Gloucester, Cirencester and Bath.

74 Dyrham Camp, also known as Hinton hill fort. *Edward J. Burrow, 'Ancient Entrenchments and Camps of Gloucestershire', 1924, p. 71*

Many historians have concluded that the Saxons may have launched a surprise attack and seized the site at Hinton Hill because it commanded the Avon Valley and disrupted communications north and south between Bath and her neighbouring towns of Gloucester and Cirencester, all three having a Roman origin. Once the Saxons were in occupation of the hill fort the Britons of those three towns were compelled to unite and make a combined attempt to dislodge them. Their attempt failed and the three opposing British kings were killed. It is probable that Roman life of some sort still existed in the three towns and the villas outside them, but with the opening up of the west of England to Saxon occupation this was extinguished. The effects of the Saxon annexation of these territories can be seen in the Latin name for two of the settlements, Glevum and Corinium, being replaced by the suffix '-cester', meaning a town or fort of Roman origin.

STRIP LYNCHETS (CENTRED ON ST 741 764)

Immediately below the Cotswold Way in the valley between Dyrham Camp and the park-wall of Dyrham are 2.2ha (5 acres) of a remarkable staircase of cultivation terraces, as well as the rectangular enclosures of an Iron Age Roman field system. (See plate 27.)

HINTON (ST 734 768)

A medieval or later shrunken village, with irregular fields extending in every direction, has been identified from aerial photographs. Earthworks on the south side of the village appear to be the remains of field boundaries, and those to the north are more likely to be the shrunken village though these have been mauled by agricultural activity. In an area made up of hamlets – settlements without parish churches – this type of desertion is common.

DYRHAM PARK (ST 741 757)

When William Blathwayt, a civil servant under James II who later became William III's acting Secretary of State, purchased the estate in the late 1680s, his intentions were to build a new house, replacing the dilapidated Tudor manor house that he found on the site. Finances dictated that a more viable option

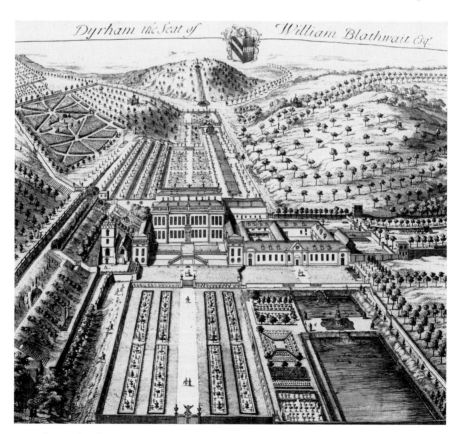

75 Dyrham Park. *Johannes Kip, 'Britannia Illustra', 1710*

would be to retain the core of the sprawling property and extend it gradually as money became available. In 1692, the new west range was started, followed by an even grander east range, then a stable block, and finally the orangery. The transformation was completed in thirteen years and Blathwayt now had an elegant baroque mansion, which was later enhanced by fabulous gardens. Both house and gardens were heavily influenced by Dutch styling, and much of the internal decor and furnishings were also of Dutch origin. Often described as having interests in the Caribbean or the sugar trade, Blathwayt did much to promote the slave trade.

The medieval deer park was created in 1620 and by 1691–1704 comprised 110ha (272 acres) of garden and rolling parkland, with spectacular, sweeping views towards Bristol. Elaborate formal gardens were laid out around the house and comprised an extensive water garden, terraces and a wilderness landscaped *c*.1800. Features include tree avenues, drives, ponds and lakes. Earlier park features include an avenue and parterres visible as earthworks and parchmarks. Romano-British features were found during recent landscaping, suggesting the extremely high probability of a major Romano-British settlement close to, or on the site of, Dyrham House.

GORSE LAND ROMAN ROAD (ST 741 377)

The 'dog leg' of the Cotswold Way route follows the Roman road between Bath and Cirencester for 100m (330ft) or so, and will do so again further on.

COLD ASHTON MANOR (ST 750726)

This building dates from the late sixteenth or early seventeenth century, and was probably built by John Gunning, Mayor of Bristol. It is listed as a Grade 1 building and is one of the best examples of the period in the country, having much Renaissance detail, although it has mainly traditional and Gothic architecture.

STRIP LYNCHETS AT COLD ASHTON (CENTRED ON ST 744 721)

This staircase of medieval strip lynchets is outstanding and one of the best preserved in the region. The features probably owe their survival to a decreasing population in the area and the abandonment of marginal land difficult to plough.

TWO ROUND BARROWS NEAR RUSHMEAD WOOD
(ST 732 704 AND ST 732 704)

The two round barrows, just visible today, were excavated in 1909 by H.H. Winwood, G. Grey and T.S. Bush. The first contained much burnt material, animal bones and potsherds, but apparently no human bones. There were numerous flints including eight scrapers and two borers. The second barrow had an unaccompanied primary cremation. A number of flints, including one borer, were found in the material of the mound. There may have been a third barrow, which was destroyed in the past.

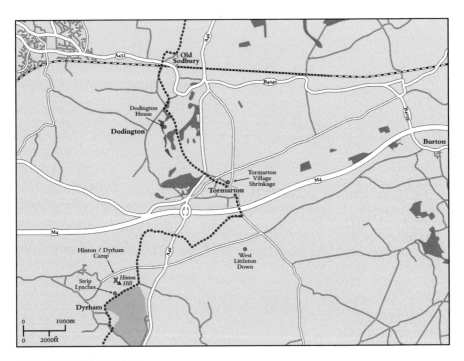

Water: Old Sodbury to Byrham.

SECTION 7

IRON, STEEL, FLINT AND GOLD
LANSDOWN TO BATH

The rounded Lansdown 'lobe' that projects from the main escarpment has sites with a long chronology, from the Mesolithic to the modern, although this density may be more apparent than real.

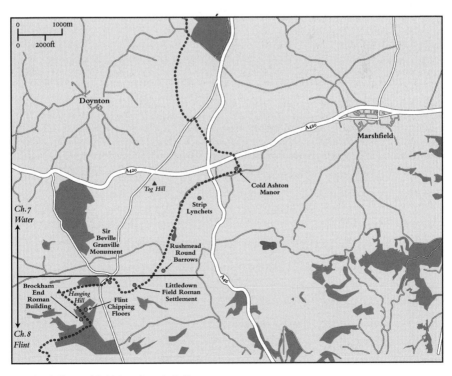

Iron, Steel, Flint and Gold: Lansdown to Bath

Besides being the site of a Civil War battle, there is an echo of the Uley with the position, age and function of the monuments, except for the presence of a long barrow. The plateau was seen as the military key to Bath and the city is clearly visible from the Prospect Stile viewpoint, especially the abbey, which is alongside the Roman Baths. It would be too easy to link these factors into producing a ritual centre, but nowhere along the trail have we encountered Roman structures at the top of the escarpment, except at the shrine at Uley.

LITTLE DOWN FIELD ROMAN SETTLEMENT (CENTRED ON ST 726 702)

The only surface features of this Roman site, marked 'settlement' with earth-works symbols on the Ordnance Survey map, are very low banks and scarps undetectable in high vegetation. Excavations from 1905 to 1908 revealed evidence of Roman occupation in the form of a two-roomed building and numerous other walls extending over the field and the next field to the west. Associated with them were Roman pottery, brooches, rings, tweezers, objects of bronze and iron, a sculptured head and about 250 coins. Seven stone coffins with skeletons, two other skeletons and a heap of skulls and bones were also unearthed. Both an Iron Age coin and pottery were found and there was evidence that an earlier wall underlay one of the Roman period. Another stone coffin was ploughed up at ST 724 702 in a 1956 excavation, which also produced 50–60 late Roman bronze coins, quantities of iron slag and moulds for shallow dishes. These moulds – including some of Oolite from the 1905–08 excavation – are now regarded as being for pewter bowls and dishes. The coin evidence shows the fourth century AD to have been the main period of occupation, and the presence of iron slag, a bone-working floor and the stone moulds indicates that the site was, at least partially, industrial. The finds would be more appropriate for a settlement around a temple than a villa.

SITE OF BATTLE (AD 1644) (ST 723 702) AND MONUMENT TO SIR BEVIL GRENVILLE (ST 721 703)

A memorial to Sir Bevil Grenville was erected in 1720 in the English Baroque style to commemorate the Royalist leader killed at the Battle of Lansdown Hill on 5 July 1643, during the English Civil War. The memorial is 7.6m (25ft) high. The lower stage has a moulded plinth and is rusticated; it bears a slate tablet with a quotation from Lord Clarendon's account of the battle.

76 Monument to Sir Bevil Grenville erected in 1720 to commemorate the Royalist leader killed at the Battle of Lansdown Hill on 5 July 1643 in the English Civil War.

The upper stage is surmounted by a griffin, which holds a shield with the Grenville coat of arms. The memorial was restored in 1777, in 1829 and again in the 1970s–80s. The location of the monument is thought to indicate the centre of the Royalist attack on the Parliamentary positions.

The Civil Wars of the mid-seventeenth century were a reflection of profound political, constitutional, religious and social conflict, which was expressed in a struggle for control between king and parliament. If the Royalists were to mount a combined attack on London, Parliamentary strength in the west had to be broken. Bath was the Parliamentary rallying point, and Lansdown Hill was the key strategic site to launch an attack on the city. Early on 5 July, the Royalists advanced on Lansdown from the north, skirmishing continuously with the Parliamentary cavalry. In the early afternoon, the Royalists stormed the Parliamentary position on the crest of the hill and forced them back to a second line of defence. Stalemate followed, neither side having the strength to finish off the other. The Parliamentarians withdrew under cover of darkness to fight another day. Bath had not fallen.

The landscape of 1643 had much in common with that of today. The plateau top was sheep pasture with arable land in less exposed areas and the steep slopes were wooded. As well as being an attractive landscape, the battlefield has a wide variety of historic features dating from the battle and earlier. Interpretation panels on the site, as well as a carefully marked battlefield trail, identify the evidence for the event – including the stone wall near the Grenville Monument, which has indications of gaps being made for muskets. The Cotswold Way route now crosses the Roman road between Bath and Cirencester encountered earlier and may have been an important factor in the location of so many Roman sites in a small area.

ENCLOSURE (ST 721 698)

The relationship of this earthwork with the Roman road is seen in the stratification: the enclosure is crossed by the road and therefore must be earlier.

The low non-defensive bank, with an outer ditch around the western half, is most likely to be an Iron Age stock enclosure, which has been dug into for stone for the road in the Roman period.

BROCKHAM END ROMAN BUILDING (ST 715 697)

When explored by the landowner in the early 1920s, three Roman-type coffins of local Oolite were found containing skeletons, one with sandal nails. Other finds included a Roman altar, an occulist's ('eye doctor') stamp and Roman pottery. Excavations in 1939 and 1946–48 produced finds of pre-Roman coins and pottery ranging from the first to fourth centuries AD. Since no indications of a wealthy, villa-type house were located, perhaps a religious context is more likely. In winter, when the undergrowth is low, fragments of dry walls at different angles can be seen with excavation trenches still visible.

FLINT CHIPPING FLOORS (CENTRED ON ST 726 694)

Collections of surface flints from a large area have been found here. The periods represented by shape and techniques used in the manufacture of the implements range from the Upper Paleolithic and Mesolithic through Neolithic to Bronze Age. These finds were made by fieldwalking when the area was ploughed rather than being the pasture golf course of today. Finds include a Paleolithic unpolished flint axe, Mesolithic microburins, and Bronze Age leaf-shaped arrowheads. The quality and geological make up of the flint suggests that it was imported through trade from the chalk areas to the south and east. If this is the case then the reasons for the siting of this settlement must be other than the location of flint in the local soils, and certainly the springs that break out further up the slopes of the valley were a determining factor. The highlands around Bath were exploited by humans from the Paleolithic onwards and the collections of flint indicate usage of this site between 8000 BC and 1000 BC. It is entirely possible that the hot springs on the valley floor of the Avon may have affected settlement for the springs could be easily visited from living sites in the uplands. The hunter-gatherers of the period before the Neolithic (and afterwards to supplement crops) would have been well aware that animals would be attracted to the springs as a source of minerals in the form of 'salt licks'. Later, the plateau would have been ideal for herding cattle or sheep. Such advantages would ensure continuity of occupation resulting in the other Bronze Age sites in the immediate area.

'ROMAN CAMP' (ST 710 691)

At this map reference in 1887, three skeletons, one in an Oolite coffin with a few small nails, were found. In 1911, during excavation a few metres from where the coffin was unearthed, a Roman occupation site consisting of several rough floors and short lengths of walling was located, though it was not possible to identify a coherent plan of a building. Brick tiles, red, grey, red and black pottery, part of a quern, an anvil or hammer stone, a flat stone and a bronze, wire armlet were also discovered. Another bronze article was considered to be the head of a Roman hairpin. The Ordnance Survey map is rather confused in this area and the 'Roman Camp' is possibly a reference to the rectangular earthwork nearby.

LITTLEDOWN CAMP (ST 709 689)

The steep climb up to this triangular, single-rampart promontory hill fort demonstrates the strong natural defences. However, the level plateau to the east necessitated a strong landward barrier, which survives as an irregular spread bank and ditch that terminates at the north and south on the escarpment, which falls away almost precipitously. The entrance is in the middle of the eastern side, which is still used in the present in the form of the Cotswold Way. There may have been a second, outside bank south of the entrance, sometimes interpreted as a round barrow. Although the irregularity of the bank may have partially resulted from stone robbing, the ditch shows different depths throughout its course, and especially between the north and south sides of the entrance way, indicating that it was unfinished.

77 Littledown Iron Age Camp. *Edward J. Burrow, 'Ancient Earthworks and Camps of Somerset', 1924*

LANSDOWN CAMP (ST 714 689)

Visible only as a low mound is an irregular, rectangular area, defined by a low, broad bank now much reduced by ploughing, except at the western end where it remains to a height of 1.2m (4ft) above the exterior. It is probably the 'Roman Camp' indicated on the Ordnance Survey maps mentioned above.

78 A rectangular earthwork on the Racecourse at Lansdown, which has been variously attributed to Roman, medieval or Civil War periods but has produced no archaeological evidence of its date. *Edward J. Burrow, 'Ancient Earthworks and Camps of Somerset', 1924*

However, evidence for a Roman structure is very tenuous, as there is no sign that the earthwork was ever square, usually the characteristic shape of a fort of that period. There are traces of a ditch along the south-eastern side and the gap here is probably an original entrance. Archaeological trenches cut in the early part of the last century revealed no evidence for the origin of the feature and while the purpose of this earthwork is uncertain, it may have even have a medieval origin.

THE LANSDOWN BARROW CEMETERY: LANSDOWN 3 (ST 711 689) AND 4 (ST 711 689)

Outside the hill fort and around the 'Roman Camp' was a series of round barrows, possibly as many as eight, forming a small cemetery. However, as the plateau top has suffered from the effects of ploughing, the construction of a golf course and the Bath Racecourse, only two survive: Lansdown 3 and 4. They now are about 6m (20ft) in diameter and perhaps on average only 1m (3ft) high. It is Lansdown 3 that is the most significant, as the find spot of a 'gold sun disc', and appropriately in summer it is covered by self-sown yellow rape flowers. (See plate 28.)

On Thursday 16 March 1905, a paper was read about excavations on Lansdown to the Society of Antiquaries at their meeting in Burlington House, London by a Fellow, A. Trice Martin, the last Headmaster of Bath College. His *Times'* obituary described him as a 'keen antiquary'.

About 200 yards [183m] to the north-west of the so-called Roman camp there are two well-marked round barrows of about 28 [8.5m] to 30 feet [9m] in diameter. The first barrow had been opened, but had certainly not been properly examined. Underneath was a circular cist about 2 feet [60cm] in diameter. This was filled with black greasy earth, resting for the most part on a 3-inch layer of stones. The bottom of the cist was reached 10 inches [24cm] lower down.

Some of the pieces of pottery are unusually thick, and it is clear that we have portions of at least two urns. The fragments of bones had all been burned, and we found some small lumps of copper, which had all been apparently fused [...] But the find of the greatest interest is the fragmentary gold-plated ornament which is far as we have been able to restore it, to be about 6 inches [15cm] in diameter [...] the fragments of the original gold plating may still be seen adhering to the bronze. We collected with the greatest care every piece, however small, that could be found. Much of the gold plating, notwithstanding all the precautions that we took, was blown away or lost. My friend Mr Grey attempted a restoration of the fragments on the theory that they represented the remains of the back of a hand-mirror, but further examination shows that they may with much greater probability be restored as a disc of which the centre consists of a circle surrounded by chevrons or rays pointing outwards. These are enclosed in a large raised circle, outside which comes a border of small raised circles, and the rim may have been fixed by copper wire hammered over the gold into a channel near the margin.

Trice Martin's change of mind about the function of the piece may have been as a result of reading about the Trundholm Sun Disc found in September 1902 in a bog in the north of Zealand in Denmark and dated to 1800–1600 BC. The motif of the sun disc has been used by many cultures; however, in Europe it indicates a belief that the sun is drawn across the heavens from east to west during the day, presenting its bright side to the earth, and returns from west to east during the night, when the dark side is being presented to the earth. The Trundholm disc is 24cm (10in) in diameter and of moulded bronze fixed

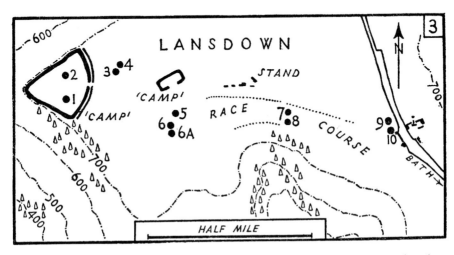

79 The distribution of round barrows on Lansdown. Barrow 3 being Trice-Martin's Barrow 1 where the 'Sun-disc' was discovered. *Audrey Williams, 'Bronze Age Barrows on Charmy Down and Lansdown, Somerset Antiquaries Journal, Vol. 30, 1959, p. 38*

vertically in the centre of an axle to which are attached two bronze wheels of four spokes, while in front is a bronze horse on four wheels attached to the rear axle by a rigid bronze bar. The disc was seen as a representation of the sun, and the likeness is emphasised by the application of gold foil by pressure to the punched surface of the bronze, while the edge was fixed by means of a copper wire hammered over the gold into a channel near the margin. A similar channel filled with copper wire occurs on the other side of the disc, which is made up of two slightly convex plates; but no gold plate was fixed to the back. Trice Martin seems to have grafted this evidence for the Trundholm Sun Disc on to the Lansdown object. (See plate 29.)

Four other 'sun discs' have been found in the England and Wales: at a round barrow at Jug's Grave in Wiltshire, two in a round barrow at Mere, Somerset, and most recently one at Cwmystwyth Mines, Ceredigion in Wales and another from Oxfordshire. Each has been about 5cm (2in) or less in diameter and has two perforations that indicated that the disc was worn attached to a garment. The lack of any visible signs of wear on their upper surfaces might imply that such objects were made specifically for burial. Each was in association with an inhumation, not a cremation such as at Lansdown. This is also true of all of the sixteen examples found in Ireland. The design of the Lansdown example has angular 'rays' originating in a circle, but the Trundholm example had circular decorations and the British and Irish ones have a cross motif.

The excavator reported that the covering stone of the cist was found slightly tilted, but apparently almost in its original position nearly in the centre of the mound. Others (including the Director of the British Museum's Antiquities Department) felt that this indicated robbing and that a horse and chariot had been removed. This raises the question of how robbers had missed the gold. If it had been robbed, then why was the gold sun disc left? If it hadn't been robbed, where were the horse and chariot? The published sections from excavation of the barrow have no indication of where the disc was found, although other drawings have a great deal of annotation. Questions of both the provenance of

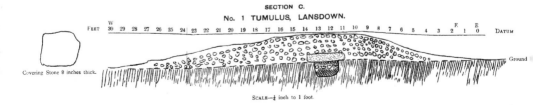

80 Trice-Martin's sketch of the 'Sun disc' barrow. Is it significant that there is no indication of the find spot of the 'Sun disc' in the section.

the 'sun disc' in the barrow and in the wider context must remain unanswered, but there is certainly room for doubt about the function of the object. Recent examination indicates that the metal composition and gilding technique are pre-Roman, but X-radiography suggests that the current positioning of the fragments is not convincing and that the replica is not entirely based on accurate observation of the existing fragments. The closest matches to the present design are on a bowl from Brandenburg in Germany and another 'sun disc' from Jaegersborg, in Jutland, Denmark.

Inevitably, after the discovery by Howard Carter in 1922 of the tomb of a now-famous pharaoh, a 1924 pamphlet by J.P.E. Falconer was entitled *Britain's Tut-ankh-amen: an account of the discovery of the burial place of a Goidelic chief near Bath*!

ROUND BARROW 6A (ST 714 686)

While constructing an extension to the racecourse in 1943, a previously unknown round barrow was discovered and excavated. It was 18m (60ft) in diameter, c.45cm (18in) high, and had a flattened top with a small crater, suggesting that it had been robbed in the past. The mound had a covered, walled cairn surrounding the centre and an extra revetment wall to stop the soil, and therefore the mound, spreading. The primary interment had been removed but the evidence indicated it had been deposited in a pit that retained charcoal, scraps of burnt bone, four small food vessel sherds, a flint flake and a broken Bronze Age flint scraper. There is now no trace of this or two other barrows close to it which were also probably destroyed when the racecourse was laid out.

PROSPECT STILE (ST 713 684)

In front of you is Kelston Round Hill, which has considerable evidence of flint knapping through the Palaeolithic period until the Bronze Age and fine strip lynchets. The North Stoke valley, with its Roman villas and Norman church, is to your right. On the left is the Italianate Beckford Monument, built in 1827 as a retreat for the writer and art collector William Beckford, where he died as a recluse with his library in 1844. Beyond is the panoramic view from Westbury in Wiltshire to the Mendip Hills, the Downs behind the City of Bath, the Avon Valley, and the hills forming the rim around the South Wales coalfield. On a good day, the Severn Bridges are visible and until the building of the first, northern, bridge in 1966 the lowest point for bridging the river was still at Gloucester. The southernmost bridge was opened in 1996 and is astride the most likely ancient river crossing point used in the prehistoric and Roman periods. The rapid ebb and flow of the tides from the River Avon to the mouth of the River Wye on the Welsh side made for a rapid, if sometimes dangerous, means of transporting people and goods. The Avon also was responsible for the growth of Bristol, an eighteenth-century slaving port. It is the wealth from this trade with the West Indies that enabled the building of some of the country houses that we have seen on the southern part of the Cotswold Way.

It's been a long way from Chipping Campden and the strong attraction of the archaeology of Bath pulls together all of the themes explored along the Cotswold escarpment. Bath was a walled small town from the Roman period until the Georgian 'boom town', when there was a tremendous and rapid explosion from the city's historic core. However, interest in the Roman and Regency periods eclipses the importance of medieval Bath. The town of the Middle Ages prospered from the woollen industry as it was ideally situated for drovers bringing their sheep in from the edge of the Cotswold Hills. As in other areas of the Cotswolds, the monastery at Bath was a considerable landowner, and the monks organised the local people to work efficiently and productively. The importance of the wool trade is illustrated by the occupations of Members of Parliament for Bath – three weavers, a cloth maker and a cloth merchant – while in Chaucer's *Canterbury Tales*, written at the end of the fourteenth century, the Wife of Bath is 'an expert in cloth making – better than the clothmakers of Ypres and Ghent'. Bath became famous for its tightly woven broadcloth and there were fifty broad looms in one area of Broad Street alone. The River Avon powered the mills and proximity to the port of Bristol helped the traders sell and export their wool and cloth, while dyes were also imported. You will finish the route very close to the East Gate, the last remaining medieval entrance, and the only extant part of the medieval city wall, thought to be on Roman foundations, is at Upper Borough Walls opposite the Royal National Hospital for Rheumatic Diseases. (See plate 30.)

While the Mendips were a source of carboniferous limestone for the lesser buildings and also the source of the lead used in Bath's plumbing, it was the Great Oolitic limestone that provided the warm honey colouring that is a distinctive feature of the city and was an important factor in its achieving World Heritage status. The underground mines at Bathampton Down and Combe Down used the 'room-and-pillar' technique, where chambers were mined and the stone between them left to support the roof. The shallowness of the mines, with 80 per cent of them being less than 6m (20ft) below the surface, has resulted in their infilling using concrete foam. Bath stone, being a 'freestone' that could be sawn or cut in any direction, was used in great quantities locally in the building of the eighteenth-century Palladian public buildings and terraces on the hillside. The attractiveness of the stone and its workability meant that it was used in nationally important structures in London as well as the provincial civic centres. Many country houses around the city were also built of Bath stone. Even where Oolitic freestones were available, as above Cheltenham, it was Bath stone that was often preferred for the fine details of ornamentation.

Water has been crucial in the development of Bath as a ritual centre and a health spa. The hot springs surfacing in the valley of the Avon originate with rain falling on the carboniferous limestone of the rim of the South Wales coalfield. The water is then forced along the joints of the limestone basin which underlies the Severn Estuary to re-appear in the Bath area, having been warmed by its journey deep in the earth. Although 'taking the waters' became an essential element in the eighteenth-century 'Bath Experience', it was the ritual and religious customs associated with the springs in the late Iron Age and the Roman period that were the foundations of the settlement of AQUAE SULIS. While the Roman temple and bath complex destroyed any trace of earlier buildings, evidence from finds, and the dedication to Celtic deity Sul and the Roman goddess Minerva, suggest the long use of a ritual landscape. Being alongside the Great Bath, or looking into the Spring, on a cold morning in winter and seeing the steam rising from the waters is an awe-inspiring experience for those of us who understand the geological processes responsible. In the past, without this knowledge, the encounter with the phenomenon must have been much more overwhelming. It cannot be a coincidence that the former Benedictine medieval monastery of Bath Abbey was built overlooking the remains of the Roman temple and baths or used stone from them. The powerful pagan forces had to be counteracted and neutralised by Christian rituals and belief.

The small Roman town of AQUAE SULIS, the 'Waters of Sul', developed primarily to serve those who undertook pilgrimage to the temple and baths complex to make their offerings to the deities of the spring. In many ways it is an appropriate place to finish the trail, as walkers along the Cotswold Way undertake a personal pilgrimage in terms of a journey or a personal search, in the case of this guide, to gain a greater understanding of the archaeological past and the peoples who created it. The Cotswold Way route has been used in parts for Christian pilgrimage, and indeed the whole trail is used today by groups prayerfully walking between the church at Chipping Campden, Hailes Abbey and Bath Abbey. However, with the original meaning of the word indicating 'a country dweller', it is good to be a 'pagan' walking along the Cotswold Edge for ten days, a week or even just a day. Enjoy!

BROADENING THE LANDSCAPE: FURTHER READING

The websites of the Bristol and Gloucestershire Archaeological Society (www.bgas.org.uk), the Gloucestershire Society for Industrial Archaeology (www.gsia.org.uk) and the Gloucester and District Archaeological Research Group (www.gadarg.org.uk) are essential sources for specific sites along most of the Cotswold Way. The southern end of the route is served by the Bath and Camerton Archaeological Society (www.bacas.org.uk) and the Somerset Archaeological and Natural History Society (www.sanhs.org). Each society publishes an annual journal.

GLOUCESTERSHIRE, SOUTH GLOUCESTERSHIRE, BATH AND NORTH EAST SOMERSET AND THE COTSWOLDS

The County of Gloucestershire was divided in 1974, with Avon subsuming the southern part as well as that of north-east Somerset, However most archaeological books tend to use the 'historic' or 'ceremonial' county as their focus. Alan Saville, The Archaeology of Gloucestershire (Cheltenham Art Gallery and Museums and BGAS, 1984), was a review of all periods and has been updated by Neil Holbrook and John Jurica's Twenty five Years of Archaeology in Gloucestershire. A Review of New Discoveries and New Thinking in Gloucestershire, South Gloucestershire and Bristol 1979–2004: Bristol and Gloucestershire Archaeological Report No 3 (Cotswold Archaeology, 2006). The most recent book on the countryside of the county is Alan S. Pilbeam, The Gloucestershire Landscape (The History Press, 2006).

An account of the archaeology of the short-lived County of Avon is contained in Michael Aston and Rob Iles' The Archaeology of Avon: A Review from the Neolithic to the Middle Ages (Avon Co. Public Relations Publicity Dept, 1987). The previous County of Avon became the counties of South Gloucestershire and Bath and North-East Somerset in 1996 and each county council's archaeology service provides an up-to-date account of recent developments in their areas.

www.gloucestershire.gov.uk/archaeology/

www.southglos.gov.uk/NR/exeres/A9C0C9E9-3B80-4147-9054-86EAF4943CB0

www.bathnes.gov.uk/services/tourism-and-heritage/archaeology

The architecture of churches, county houses and villages is described in Nicholas Pevsner's Buildings of England series (1999): Gloucestershire: the Cotswolds and (2002) Somerset North and Bristol, both published by Yale University Press.

Two highly important recent initiatives are an archaeological aerial survey in the Cotswold Hills, www.english-heritage.org.uk/publications/archaeological-aerial-survey-cotswold-hills-nmp/4755_Cotswold_Hills_NMP_Report.pdf, and the use of LiDAR (Light

Detection And Ranging) along the Cranham area of the route of the Cotswold Way: see Diane Charlesworth and Les Comtesse's *Seeing Through the Trees, the Cotswold Edge LiDAR project* (Gloucester and District Archaeological Research Group, 2010)

GEOLOGY

www.naturalengland.org.uk/ourwork/conservation/geodiversity/englands/counties/area_ID13.asp.
Dreghorn, W., *Geology Explained in the Forest of Dean and Wye Valley* (Fineleaf Publications, 2005)

ARCHAEOLOGY

Aston, Michael, *Interpreting the Landscape: Landscape Archaeology and Local History* (Routledge, 1985)
Hoskins, W.G., *The making of the English landscape* (Hodder and Stoughton, 2005)
Muir, Richard, *Landscape Encyclopaedia* (Windgather Press, 2004)
Muir, Richard, *Woods, Hedges and Leafy Lanes* (The History Press, 2008)
Pryor, Francis, *The Making of the British Landscape: How We Have Transformed the Land From Prehistory to Today* (Penguin, 2011)

Prehistory

Cunliffe, Barry, *Britain Begins* (Oxford University Press, 2012)
Darvill, Timothy, *Prehistoric Gloucestershire: Forest and Vales and High Blue Hills* (Amberley Publishing, 2009)
Darvill, Timothy, *Prehistoric Britain* (Routledge, 2010)
Pryor, Francis, *Britain BC: Life in Britain and Ireland Before the Romans* (Harper Perennial, 2004)

Long Barrows

Darvill, Timothy, *Long Barrows of the Cotswolds* (The History Press, 2004)
Smith, Martin and Brickley, Megan, *People of the Long Barrows* (The History Press, 2009)
There has been no recent book specifically about round barrows but lists of the sites in Gloucestershire by O'Neil, Helen and Grinsell, L.V., in 1960 are online at www2.glos.ac.uk/bgas/tbgas/v079/bg079099.pdf, with an update by Grinsell, L.V. and Darvill T.C. in 1989 at www2.glos.ac.uk/bgas/tbgas/v107/bg107039.pdf
Again, there is no recent account of hill forts along the Cotswold Way, but Ralston, Ian, *Celtic Fortifications* (The History Press, 2006) and Brown, Ian, *Beacons in the Landscape: the hill forts of England and Wales* (Windgather Press, 2008) are useful overviews. Cunliffe, Barry, *Danebury Hill Fort* (The History Press, 2011) describes the results of the most extensive excavation of a hill fort in Britain.

The Roman period

Bird, Stephen and Cunliffe, Barry, *The Essential Roman Baths* (Scala Publications, 2006)
Copeland, Tim, *Roman Gloucestershire* (The History Press, 2011)
Cunliffe, Barry, *Roman Bath Discovered* (The History Press, 2000)
De la Bédoyère, Guy, *Roman Britain: A New History* (Thames and Hudson, 2010)
Russell, Miles and Laycock, Stuart, *Exposing the Great Myth of Britannia* (The History Press, 2011)

The medieval period

There has been no recent survey of the whole medieval archaeology of England, though Aston (1985) and Hoskins (2005) cited above in archaeology deal largely with the medieval countryside.

Aston, Mick, *Monasteries in the Landscape* (Tempus, 2000)

Davenport, Peter, *Medieval Bath Uncovered* (The History Press, 2002)

Hurst, Derek, *Sheep in the Cotswolds: The Medieval Wool Trade* (The History Press, 2005)

Rodwell, Warwick, *The Archaeology of Churches* (Amberley Publishing, 2012)

The industrial period

The Gloucester Society for Industrial Archaeology's Annual Journal is indispensible for this period.

Handford, Michael and Viner, David, *Stroudwater and Thames and Severn Canal* (The History Press, 2009)

Jowett, David and Attwood, Richard, *Cotswold Canals: An Introduction to the Stroudwater Navigation and the Thames and Severn Canal* (Cotswold Canal Trust, 2009)

Mills, Stephen, *The Mills of Gloucestershire* (Barracuda, 1989)

Mills, Stephen, Riemer, Pierce, Standing, Ian and Wilson, Ray, *A Guide to the Industrial Archaeology of Gloucestershire* (Association for Industrial Archaeology, 1992)

Tann, Jennifer, *Wool and Water: Gloucestershire Woollen Industry and Its Mills* (The History Press, 2012)

The Second World War and the Cold War periods

Dalton, Mark, *The Royal Observer Corps Underground Posts* (Folly Books, 2011)

Green, M., *War Walks: Stop Line Green* (Reardon Publishing, 1999)

Osbourne, Mike, *Twentieth Century Structures in the Landscape* (The History Press, 2004)

INDEX